C000235940

A PRACTICAL GUIDE TO
CLASSROOM
RESEARCH

A PRACTICAL GUIDE TO
CLASSROOM
RESEARCH

CLIVE MILLAR

First published in 2016 by Critical Publishing Ltd

British Library Cataloguing in Publication Data
A CIP record for this book is available from the British Library

ISBN: 978-1-911106-36-4

This book is also available in the following e-book format:
MOBI: 978-1-911106-37-1

Cover and text design by Out of House Ltd
Project Management by Out of House Publishing Solutions
Typeset by Newgen Knowledge Works Pvt. Ltd.
Print Managed and Manufactured by Jellyfish Solutions

Critical Publishing
152 Chester Road
Northwich
CW8 4AL
www.criticalpublishing.com

MIX
Paper from
responsible sources
FSC   FSC® C013056
www.fsc.org

In memory of Donald McIntyre

Help us to help you

Our aim is to help you to become the best professional you can be. In order to improve your critical thinking skills we are pleased to offer you a **free booklet** on the subject.

Just go to our website www.criticalpublishing.com and click the link on the home page.

We have more free resources on our website which you may also find useful.

If you'd like to write a review of this book on Amazon, Books Etc., or Wordery, **we would be happy to send you the digital version of the book for free.**

Email a link to your review to us at admin@criticalpublishing.com, and we'll reply with a PDF of the book, which you can read on your phone, tablet or Kindle.

You can also connect with us on:

Twitter   @CriticalPub #criticalpublishing
Facebook   www.facebook.com/Critical-Publishing-456875584333404
Our blog   https://thecriticalblog.wordpress.com

Contents

Meet the author

Clive Millar taught English at high schools in Cape Town and in rural Scotland. He became a lecturer at Aberdeen College of Education and at the University of Cape Town, Professor of Education at the University of Fort Hare, and Professor of Adult Education and Director of Extra-mural Studies at the University of Cape Town until his early retirement in 1998. His research on micro-teaching at the University of Stirling was supervised by Donald McIntyre, who became a lifelong friend. He was invited to introduce a course in classroom research at the Centre for Creative Education in Cape Town and has enjoyed doing this for the last ten years. He lives in deep retirement with his wife, Sheila, above the sea in Scarborough, the most south-westerly village in Africa. He is blessed with five grandchildren, all living close by.

He would welcome comments on his book and its approach to research. His email address is seamillars@gmail.com.

Acknowledgements

When the idea for this book arose, I wrote the following letter to the students in my class of 2015:

Dear Research Students of 2015

When I introduced you to the mysteries of qualitative research at the beginning of 2015 I didn't know that you would be the last class I would teach at the Centre for Creative Education. I have, unfortunately, become too weak to tackle the task again this year though I am still able to supervise a few students.

Very recently, to fill an intellectual vacuum, I decided to explore writing a book, or rather a guidebook. This would be on qualitative classroom research, and it would draw on my experience of teaching and supervising research at CCE over the last ten years. I am glad to say that this book is slowly beginning to take shape.

I am writing to you to ask your permission to make use of some of the things you wrote on your research journeys and in your final research reports. They would be used as examples and illustrations in my text, and would hopefully add some vitality to the guidebook. I would acknowledge your contribution, of course, but ensure that any quotes from your work were anonymous or disguised by pseudonyms.

Please let me know if you would wish to help me in this way. Our collective research journey in 2015 was a particularly happy and successful one, and I would like to see it come to life again in this way.

Warm wishes
Prof

I wish to thank these students for giving their permission with such enthusiasm. I will be delighted if, through this guide, their work is able to reach a wider audience.

I wish to thank, too:

My colleagues at the Centre for Creative Education for their consistent support of my attempts to improve the quality of student research and for their permission to make use of materials developed for the Centre.

My wise and inspiring editor, Julia Morris, with whom it has been such fun to work.

My family and friends: Barry Hymer, Christine Findlay and especially Sheila, who encouraged me to write the book and supported me all the way.

Clive Millar, 2016

Foreword

Clive Millar has produced an exciting introductory course in classroom research and a tried and tested method for supervising the production of student research reports. The course and method have both emerged from the authority of his experience of some ten years of working to improve his own support for classroom research in the Centre for Creative Education in Cape Town. The book is published by Critical Publishing and it is the balance between the exercise of the creativity of individuals and being critical in beginning classroom research that provides the uniqueness of this text.

Clive Millar's hope is that you will use this book as an accessible and practical guide to the research process, both from beginning to end; and as a resource to dip into when you are faced with specific problems or queries. The excitement for me, in reading this text, is in both his conception of research – "*as a slowly developing investigation driven by a question that will lead to theoretical answers with practical implications*" – that the novice researcher has to imagine and learn, and the pedagogical processes, with a supervisor, that can lead a beginning researcher to produce an accredited research report within four months.

Students were required to become writers from the first moment of the research module. The pressure to write was relentless. To begin with, what was written was examined, critiqued and improved in class. Then, after two weeks, all writing was submitted and critiqued by email with a 24 hour turn-around time. Research teacher became research supervisor. Though there were strict deadlines for each draft chapter students could send small sections for comment whenever they wished to. All supervision was by email. There were no meetings. All conversation was both *in* writing and *about* writing.

If you are a student beginning your classroom research this book gives practical examples of how you can engage, as a group and individually, with a series of real tasks that are achievable within a relatively short time. The crucial advice is focused on your writing. It is vital for research that your systematic enquiry is made public so that it is open to validation, can contribute to the knowledge-base and enhance professionalism in education. The book shows how every small piece of your writing can and should be made public as a stage in the completion of the task of enabling your research report to become a reality.

If you are a supervisor of a beginner researcher the book shows how you can support a researcher to find their researcher voice. The book stresses the importance of forming an answerable question, with practical examples. It demonstrates how data can be gathered through interviews, observation and conversation and analysed in terms of an answer to the research question.

Beginning researchers and supervisors are shown how research reports can be completed in three chapters:

> **Chapter 1 was a genuine research plan, written before immersion in the research site. Chapter 2 reported on the actual implementation of this research plan. And Chapter 3 reflected on the significance of the data reported on in Chapter 2. Each chapter was enabled by, and built on, the previous one. And each acknowledged and addressed the limitations of the previous one.**

The uniqueness and importance of this text is its evidence-base in demonstrating how a beginning researcher and a supervisor can work together to produce an accredited research report within four months. The book includes the criteria and marking scheme for the accreditation.

In a section on the integration of the introductory research module and school-based research we are provided with the evidence that shows how a two-week research module at the start of the final year flowed directly into school-based research. This module enabled students to write the first chapter of their research reports and submit this in draft form within a week after the module ended.

> **The second chapter was due three weeks later, and the final chapter two weeks after this. Further research classes were scheduled to support this process. This procedure enabled the research course to be relevant (in "real time") to each of the three stages students were going through in their research process – *planning and design, data collection and organisation*, and *analysis and discussion*. This was a form of concentration in time and an integration of what had been separate components was the key innovation.**

Another strength of the text is the way it shows how beginning researchers can be encouraged to engage creatively and critically with the ideas of others in the generation of their own research accounts of answering their questions. The focus on the generation of research accounts serves to emphasize the importance of the beginning researchers as knowledge-creators. This had profound implications for a global movement to enhance professionalism in education. Clive Millar has drawn on his own embodied knowledge as a professional educator to produce a book that focuses on the bedrock of enhancing research-based professionalism in education. This is the bedrock of encouraging beginning researchers to engage in classroom research as knowledge creators who can explain their educational influences in their own learning and in the learning of others and contribute their research accounts to the knowledge-base of education. I do hope that you enjoy the book as much as I have enjoyed reading it and writing this foreword.

Jack Whitehead
Visiting Professor in Education, University of Cumbria

Endorsement

There are many good texts for classroom-based researchers, but few that manage to distil the challenges and component parts of engaging in good research in the classroom with such lucidity. This is a book that is simple without being join-the-dots simplistic, and its parsimony will be attractive to teachers needing to integrate their research into the great workload of their daily practice and who don't have the time or headspace to engage in the rarefied debates in which the field abounds (and from which it benefits). That said, it is a feature of this book that it doesn't deny or ignore the infinite and inevitable messiness of social research. On the contrary, it positively revels in these, and uses real-life examples to illustrate salient elements of the research process. To cap it all, the author's command and love of language imbues this book with an admirable elegance and accessibility. It deserves to become the go-to book for early-career teacher–researchers.

Barry Hymer
Professor of Psychology in Education, University of Cumbria

Introduction

This book is both a guide to qualitative classroom research and an extended case study of how a particular group of college students conducted and successfully completed empirical investigations in several classrooms – because abstract advice needs to be backed up with the study of concrete examples.

The guide provides access to a real research journey by a small group of student researchers. It is a step-by-step account of how qualitative classroom research was carried out and completed over a four-month period. Each stage in the case study is followed by a statement of guidelines applicable to a range of similar investigations into classroom practice.

The focus of the guide is on crafting and writing a research report. I have used the term 'research report' in preference to 'dissertation' or 'thesis' because it is less pretentious, suggests a relatively brief document, and stresses the past-tense nature of the writing. This is a report on work that has been carried out.

The book began with an invitation ten years ago to introduce a research component into the final year of a four-year undergraduate teacher education programme at a small private college. I was given considerable freedom to develop, through trial and error, both an introductory course in classroom research and a method of supervising the production of student research reports. I have drawn on this experience in this guide.

If you are reading this you are probably a college, university or school-based student engaged in the study of education, at an advanced undergraduate or postgraduate level. You may be full-time or part-time, and you may be studying face-to-face or by distance learning, but your programme will probably require a formal research report or dissertation. You could also be a beginning teacher responding to the drive for greater evidence-based teaching in classrooms. Whatever your situation, you are likely to have a particular interest in classroom research – in investigating in some depth and detail what goes on in the real world of a particular classroom.

My hope is that you will use this book as an accessible and practical guide to the research process, from beginning to end; and as a resource to dip into when you are faced with specific problems or queries.

1 Becoming a researcher

How can I tell what I think till I see what I say?

E M Forster (1927, p 101)

BEGINNING WITH IMAGINATION

A research project begins in the imagination – imagining what research is, what a research report looks like and what it means to be a researcher. And students do not easily imagine themselves as researchers. Of all academic tasks, research is the most intimidating. It is often surrounded in mystique and seen as demanding and difficult. Can I do this? Will I succeed in writing a good research report? These are common questions in the first stages of the research process.

A week into their introductory course in research methods (a course that required students to begin writing their research plans from the first morning), I asked one of my classes to give a brief answer (anonymously) to the following question: *What have you learnt about yourself during the past few days?*

Their answers reflect considerable anxiety. Imagining oneself as a researcher is no easy task.

I struggle to move forward (or write) when I am uncertain. I worry about failing the task.

I lack concentration when I get too stressed and overthink or analyse too in depth.

I panic far too easily and worry when there is actually no need for worry because we are all in the same boat. Taking deep breaths helps! There is help if I need it but I hardly ever ask for it.

I have learnt that I am not nearly as willing to make mistakes and put myself (intellectually) out there as I thought I was.

I have learnt that I am quite concerned with appearing to be intelligent. I have felt a lot of pressure but now that I have recognised this I feel more relaxed and am better able to just be me without keeping up appearances.

> *The big fear I have about writing a research report is that I feel very uncertain and that when I am criticised it makes me lose confidence and I feel more uncertain than before. I cannot imagine submitting the final document.*

At the same time, however, positive strategies and attitudes are taking shape – ways of thinking about doing research and being a researcher. Students are talking themselves into the role of researcher; imagining what this may require of them. The process of becoming a researcher has begun. Students are saying to themselves, in very different ways, 'I can do this'.

> *I have learned that I can go beyond my limits and take on something that is totally foreign to me, if I put thought and much effort into it.*
>
> *I have learned that this work requires of me a 'push' of intellectual and physical work within a specified time.*
>
> *I have learned that I have a strong sense of perseverance. I have realised I can trust the theory of 'it'll come' and 'sleep on it'.*
>
> *I have learned that I enjoy taking in people's thoughts and ideas. Pieces of a puzzle coming together that may or may not ever be finished.*
>
> *I have discovered that I am deeply passionate about writing and philosophising – it energises and inspires me in ways I never dreamed possible. I realise too – I tend to struggle following an idea or train of thought to its conclusion – am prone to confusion and emotional conflict and anxiety. But that's okay.*
>
> *I need to develop and 'exercise' my own imagination in order to be the teacher/ researcher/writer I want to be. That I am more interested (for now) in researching teaching, than actually teaching... or maybe that I am uncomfortable with the often dissonant space between theory and practice.*

These students are taking key steps in imagining themselves as researchers; they are reflecting on their personal experience of beginning to think like researchers and imagining, too, what they might need to do in order to succeed in the task. They are also drawing some comfort from being part of a group of fellow travellers.

DIFFERENT CONCEPTIONS OF RESEARCH

False stereotypes of research

One of the problems faced by novice researchers is that they may have to unlearn intuitive and common-sense understandings of what research is. The first misleading idea is that research is about *collecting information*. Collecting information is part of research but not the central part. The second is that a research report is a kind of *essay*. Students are accustomed to essay and collection modes of writing and might easily assume that research involves simply the collection of information and its presentation in essay form.

What both these stereotypes miss is the key feature of research: that it is a process of systematic inquiry directed by a question that has no simple answer. It is this conception of research – *as a slowly developing investigation driven by a question that will lead to theoretical answers with practical implications* – that the novice researcher has to imagine and learn.

Quantitative and qualitative research traditions

Established approaches to research fall into two major traditions: quantitative and qualitative.

- *Quantitative research* rests on the measurement of variables and the search for relationships among variables using statistical procedures. It is the classic procedure of mainstream science. Its use is pervasive: in opinion polls, in drug trials, in comparing crop yields, in all the physical sciences. It includes large-scale surveys of various kinds as well as controlled experiments. The data generated reveal correlations between variables; and may in some cases clarify cause and effect. Findings are usually generalisable.
- *Qualitative research*, by contrast, is confined largely to the social sciences. It makes no attempt to define and quantify the factors or variables to be examined. Its approach is exploratory: it attempts to understand what is happening in natural situations, drawing on participants' intuitive understandings. Its main methods are observation and interview. The findings of qualitative research are not generalisable to other situations. This does not mean that they cannot provide insight into other situations.

The following comparative table produced by Xavier University Library (2012) puts the distinctions between these two traditions in clear and useful terms.

Table 1.1 Qualitative versus quantitative research: a comparative table (Xavier University Library, 2012)

Criteria	Qualitative research	Quantitative research
Purpose	To understand and interpret social interactions.	To test hypotheses, look at cause and effect, and make predictions.
Group studied	Smaller and not randomly selected.	Larger and randomly selected.
Variables	Study of the whole, not variables.	Specific variables studied.
Type of data collected	Words, images or objects.	Numbers and statistics.
Form of data collected	Qualitative data such as open-ended responses, interviews, participant observations, field notes and reflections.	Quantitative data based on precise measurements using structured and validated data collection instruments.
Type of data analysis	Identify patterns, features and themes.	Identify statistical relationships.
Objectivity and subjectivity	Subjectivity is expected.	Objectivity is critical.
Role of the researcher	Researcher and their biases may be known to participants in the study, and participant characteristics may be known to the researcher.	Researcher and their biases are not known to participants in the study, and participant characteristics are deliberately hidden from the researcher (double blind studies).
Results	Particular or specialised findings that are less generalisable.	Generalisable findings that can be applied to other populations.
Scientific method	Exploratory or bottom-up: the researcher generates a new hypothesis and theory from the data collected.	Confirmatory or top-down: the researcher tests the hypothesis and theory with the data.
View of human behaviour	Dynamic, situational, social and personal.	Regular and predictable.
Most common research objectives	Explore, discover and construct.	Describe, explain and predict.
Focus	Wide-angle lens; examines the breadth and depth of phenomena.	Narrow-angle lens; tests a specific hypothesis.

Table 1.1 (*cont.*)

Criteria	Qualitative research	Quantitative research
Nature of observation	Study behaviour in a natural environment.	Study behaviour under controlled conditions; isolate causal effects.
Nature of reality	Multiple realities; subjective.	Single reality; objective.
Final report	Narrative report with contextual description and direct quotations from research participants.	Statistical report with correlations, comparisons of means and statistical significance of findings.

Xavier University Library acknowledges that content in the above table was taken from the following sources: Johnson, B and Christensen, L (2008) *Educational Research: Quantitative, Qualitative, and Mixed Approaches*. Thousand Oaks, CA: Sage Publications, p 34; Lichtman, M (2006) *Qualitative Research in Education: A User's Guide*. Thousand Oaks, CA: Sage Publications, pp 7–8.

QUALITATIVE CLASSROOM RESEARCH

Why is qualitative research the appropriate approach for classroom research – for exploring social interaction in classrooms? There are several reasons for this.

The nature of classrooms

The first reason is to do with the nature of classrooms. Primary school classrooms, for example, have a lot in common but each is, at the same time, unique. Each is a small but complex social world, requiring constant interpretation and challenging the teacher's understanding. Teachers and children are active creators and negotiators of what goes on in their classrooms. What things mean to them is of primary importance. The key question in qualitative research – 'What is happening here?' – is a question that needs to be asked again and again in the daily life of classrooms.

Furthermore, there are ethical reasons for viewing the classroom as a natural situation to be understood rather than a site for an experiment or the measurement of variables. Children and teachers are actors whose motives and meanings have to be respected, engaged with and understood through language and observation rather than measured within predetermined categories.

The purpose of classroom research

The second reason why qualitative research is an appropriate approach is to do with the purpose and context of classroom research. Its purpose is to deepen understanding of some aspect of learning and teaching; its hope is that such understanding will inform improved practice. The main beneficiary of such research will be the researcher, whether he or she is the teacher of the class being studied or possibly intends to become a teacher. Classroom research is usually practitioner research. It implies a deepened professionalism for the teacher: a commitment to researching one's own practice.

The teacher as researcher

A key characteristic of what has been seen as a deepened form of professionalism is the capacity and commitment to reflect on one's own practice. The most famous expression of this idea was the term 'reflective practitioner', the focus of Donald Schön's influential book, *The Reflective Practitioner: How Professionals Think In Action* (Schön, 1983). He saw critical self-reflection as a defining characteristic of a practitioner, in any professional field, who is committed to developing his or her craft by learning from experience.

The term 'teacher–researcher' was used by Lawrence Stenhouse in his classic argument that classroom teaching should be seen as research-based practice (Stenhouse, 1975). He saw systematic reflection by teachers as the crucial means of professional development and of creative innovation in classrooms. Much of Donald McIntyre's later work, building on this tradition, was concerned with the systematic, collaborative development of 'professional craft knowledge' by teachers through study and reflection on day-to-day practice. See *Learning Teaching from Teachers* (Hagger and McIntyre, 2006).

Classroom research in teacher education

The idea of developing 'reflective practitioners' – teachers who think about what they do and why they do it – lies behind the decision to introduce research components into teacher education programmes. It is not sufficient to induct student teachers into 'good practice'; they need to learn to critique good practice, to think on their feet in unpredictable situations and to grow professionally through reflection on practice.

The important thing is that a qualitative approach begins with participants' intuitive understandings of the situations in which they find themselves. It does not displace these common-sense understandings with 'better', more objective or scientific ones. It respects where teachers are and gives them the skills and security to examine, critique and build on their early taken-for-granted assumptions.

FINDING A RESEARCHER VOICE:
'MY RESEARCHER VOICE CAME ALONG SILENTLY'

Students are often resistant to committing themselves to thought on paper. They prefer to talk than to write. In the research course for student teachers I draw on in writing this book, students were expected to become writers from the first morning.

The pressure to write was relentless. To begin with, what was written was examined, critiqued and improved in class. Then, after two weeks, all writing was submitted to their research supervisor and critiqued by email with a 24-hour turnaround time. There were no meetings. All conversation was in writing and about writing.

After three weeks of work, when their drafts of Chapter 1 of the research report had been submitted, I sent students the following invitation:

Finding your voice as a researcher

Over the past three weeks you have done an amazing thing: you have learned to become a researcher. Okay, some of you were already close, but others were light-years away. Some found it mysteriously easy; others incredibly difficult. But you all, in one way or another, have found, or are finding, your voice as a researcher. And some of you have had to learn a new writing style too: formal, academic English. You have made remarkable progress. And I don't really understand how it all happened.

So a new research question is taking shape in my mind (or rather the very oldest and best qualitative research question is taking shape): What is happening here? What has been happening here? How on earth do we find our voices as researchers? And learn to write in an academic way?

You are the only people able to answer these questions. Will you try?

The three students quoted below had no previous experience of the conventions of formal academic writing.

My researcher voice came along silently without me even realising this was happening. I did not give the 'researcher voice' much thought as I was (still am) focusing on my writing and writing style. I could only follow and notice my researcher voice after I completed chapter one but not during.

Working through previous fourth year students' research reports gives us a feel for what is expected and the manner in which to write a research report. Reading through multiple students' research reports is a good way to begin finding your own style of writing. Finding a style that you are comfortable with and a style that suits your research is important.

I found that the best solution to transform my informal writing to formal/academic writing was to get an editor or somebody who has a proper grasp on formal writing to help you. Sitting down with my sister-in-law has helped me majorly. She has been patient and guided me in a way that aided me to correct my own mistakes and to write in a more academic style.

In order to find your research voice, you need to research something you are interested in. You will not develop a researcher's voice if you research something that you don't want to. It will result in a boring and dull research report. Researching something that intrigues you hopefully should result in attention-grabbing research. To develop a researcher's voice you need to write with feeling and passion and express your opinions and thoughts. This becomes easy if you research something that fascinates you.

This process has been overwhelming for me; I don't think it was just the level of difficulty but more so the limit of time we've been given. Maybe working under pressure forces one's ability to think quickly and get the 'job' done knowing there is a much needed deadline and the significance of completing our thesis.

Finding our voice certainly comes with experience and actively being involved in the process; reflecting, keeping up, asking questions when unsure during the process etc. It almost happens subliminally because we are, in a way, forced to become a researcher and along the way we start thinking like one and reflecting it into speech and writing.

These insights are both insightful and practical. Certainly, these students are learning to be researchers through writing like researchers. But they are also learning through serious reflection on the process they are going through. The engine for both processes is being faced with a real and immediate task: writing their research plans – the first chapter of their research report – and having three weeks in which to do this.

WRITING YOURSELF INTO THE RESEARCH PROCESS

If you have not written in research mode before, you will need to find your 'researcher voice' – a style of writing that is both appropriate for the research task and authentic for you. For most students, this is probably something that 'comes along silently'. It emerges as a by-product of ongoing work.

In this section, I argue that we 'write ourselves into the research process'. We need to see ourselves as writers and make writing the cutting edge of our task. Such writing is a form of thinking aloud. It is a developing commentary on the research process. It is the earliest draft of the research report. And it needs to be a simple, honest record of ongoing thinking, something like the following:

I think my research focus will be on some aspect of classroom discussion. I am interested in why some discussions 'work' and are interesting and involving, and others do not. But I don't yet have a clear enough focus.

My tentative research question is taking shape. But it remains far too vague. This is my question at present…

We may write for an interested supervisor, for one or two supportive peers perhaps, but above all for ourselves. '*How can I tell what I think till I see what I say?*', as E M Forster (1927, p 101) put it.

The enemy of research report writing is deferral, of not being quite ready to commit thoughts to paper. The rule is not to wait for perfection, but rather to describe in simple narrative your engagement with the research task, step by step. Slowly, in this way, a draft of the research report is crafted.

WHO SAYS RESEARCH IS AN INTELLECTUAL PROCESS?

It is certainly an intellectual process but it is as much an emotional experience. It draws on all one's confidence, courage, resilience, humour and doggedness. Research, like old age, is not for sissies. It requires stance and style – attitude – and such things are not under neat intellectual management.

This is why the institutional context of the researcher is so important – the availability of good, caring support structures, formally and informally. It is striking how many students, on the completion of their research reports, comment on the stress of the process and give priority to thanking those who have supported them in personal ways on their journey. Family members and fellow students are thanked for 'understanding, patience and moral support'; supervisors for 'encouragement and kind words in times of defeat and angst that always lifted the spirit'. It is emotional rather than intellectual support that is stressed.

SUMMARY OF KEY POINTS

- Start to view yourself as a researcher.

- Research is not just about collecting information.

- Research is systematic inquiry directed by a complex question.

- Research can be qualitative or quantitative.

- Qualitative research lends itself well to the classroom.

- Write yourself into a researcher mindset.

- Research is both intellectual and emotional.

2 A research report format: having a destination and a route

It is good to have an end to journey toward; but it is the journey that matters, in the end.

Ursula Le Guin (1969, p 220)

INTRODUCTION

This chapter stresses the importance of having a clear sense of the shape of a final research report as well as a route and timetable to reach this destination. It works through the following sequence of topics:

*   the purpose of a research report format;
*   the four key stages of the research report;
*   a discussion of the requirements of each stage;
*   how the format can become a timetable.

THE PURPOSE OF A FORMAT

At a very early stage in the research process it helps to have a *format* in mind for the final report: it provides a goal to aim for and a degree of security. The scope of the report has been defined, its components listed, and you have a sense of what your final research report might look like. The format I introduce below will not survive the research journey without alteration, but it will provide a useful sense of destination with which to begin it. See it as a sketch map of the possible shape of the destination, seen from a high altitude.

At first glance, proposing a format to structure the writing of a research report looks like a highly restrictive move. And in a sense it is. But having a format in mind seems to me a necessary restriction, especially for novice researchers. A format is a practical way of taking formal conventions seriously. There is no contradiction between respecting formal frameworks and producing imaginative and original research. I think the examples of research students' work that follow will make this clear. A classical apprenticeship has equipped many a jazz musician.

A further important reason for having a format in advance is that, however sketchily, this format communicates something of the systematic process of inquiry that research requires. In so doing, it may begin to contest the intuitive, common-sense templates that beginning researchers inevitably own, misconceptions that reduce research to collecting information, summarising information or writing an essay. See this second function of the format as providing a simple route map towards the destination.

THE FOUR KEY STAGES OF THE RESEARCH REPORT

A research project goes through four stages:

1. Research planning and design.
2. Reporting on the implementation of the plan: a review of the research process.
3. The summary of research data.
4. Analysis and conclusion.

A full account of these four stages is essential for an adequate research report. Below, stage by stage, I suggest a simple format for doing this. (In Appendix 1 you will find this format arranged in chapter form.)

Stage 1: research planning and design

RESEARCH PLANNING AND DESIGN

1. *The research theme*: Give a brief introduction to your research theme and explain why you think it is worth investigating.
2. *Preliminary reading*: Give an outline of what you have learnt about your research theme through preparatory reading. Explain which ideas you have found most interesting and useful in helping you to define your research question.
3. *The research question*: Define your research question clearly and explain how you arrived at it.
4. *Research design*: Describe and justify the qualitative research approach chosen for your investigation; and explain and justify the particular research methods you have chosen to use.
5. *Research site(s)*: Describe your proposed research site(s) and subjects. Given your particular research question, what do you see as the advantages as well as the possible limitations of your research site?
6. *Research ethics*: Identify the ethical issues you see arising in your particular investigation and explain how you intend to deal with them.
7. *Purposes and expectations*: Clarify the theoretical purposes of your research (what it is you wish to understand?), its practical purposes (ways in which your findings might prove useful) and its personal purposes (possible benefits to you individually).

Discussion

Although this first stage of the research report is about planning and design, I suggest you write it as a chapter in the past tense, seeing it as a *retrospective narrative* report on how you carried out the planning and design stage.

The *sequence* of the seven steps is to an extent logical.

- The *research theme* introduces and focuses the report.
- The *preliminary reading* section explores this theme and explains the route taken to define the *research question*.
- The *research question* section defines and explains the key question directing the investigation.
- The *research design* section explains how the investigation will be carried out: how the data required to answer this question will be gathered.
- Given this design, the *research site* section assesses the advantages and limitations of the chosen site.
- The final two sections require a clarification of ethical guidelines and an assessment of the possible benefits of the project.

The format is also roughly *chronological*. The intention is that the order in which the report is written should reflect the logical sequence.

Stage 2: the implementation of the research plan

The second stage of the format for the report deals with the implementation of the research plan: an account of how the *research process* was carried out in practice.

REVIEW OF THE RESEARCH AND DATA COLLECTION PROCESS

Report briefly on how the research was carried out in practice. Give a clear account of how you implemented your research plan, including problems encountered and improvisations required. The following sub-headings might be useful:

- How you organised access to your research site.

- How you carried out the interviewing process, how you used your interview guides and how you recorded and processed your data.

- How you carried out the observation process, how you used your observation guides and how you recorded and processed your data.

- How you attempted to ensure the accuracy of your data.

- How the research question might have changed or developed during the data collection process.

- Ethical issues and how you dealt with these.

- The strengths and limitations that emerged in your research plan.

Discussion

The review of the research process is an account of how the implementation of the research plan was carried out in practice. Once again, it is a narrative report. I suggest that it is written largely in the past tense, probably with brief shifts into the present tense where this seems appropriate.

This review includes *six areas* that should be reported on: access to the research site; observation, interviewing and recording procedures; accuracy of data; possible pressures on the research question; ethical issues; and an assessment of the practicality of the research plan.

The aim of such a review of process is to provide a critical reader with a clear account of the conditions under which the research data was generated. The practicalities of carrying out this review are discussed in Chapter 8.

Stage 3: the summary of research data

The data summary is a crucial step in the development of the research report. The format includes only the barest of guidelines for structuring this summary. This process, too, will be examined in some detail in Chapter 9.

SUMMARY OF RESEARCH DATA

Present a well-organised summary (including brief quotations where appropriate) of your research data. You will need to consider the most useful way to structure this summary. Your research question and your interview and observation guides will help you to do this.

Stage 4: analysis and conclusion

The final part of the proposed format is *analysis and conclusion*. This can be seen as the culmination of the research report.

ANALYSIS AND CONCLUSION

Interpret your data in a systematic, reflective and open-minded way, supporting conclusions with reference to the data. You may wish to draw on additional theoretical reading to assist you with this.

Indicate what questions require further investigation; identify possible applications of research findings; and reflect briefly on your intellectual journey.

Only the briefest guideline is suggested here. It is not advisable to recommend any detailed format for this crucial section of the research report. The last thing one wants at this crucial stage is a neat prescription that restricts thought and imagination. The complex task of analysis is dealt with in some detail in Chapter 10.

THE FOUR-STAGE FORMAT: USE AND LIMITATIONS

The above four-stage format is a suggestion for giving practical form, at an early stage, to the requirements of a formal research report. It provides a picture of a visible destination. And it breaks down what might seem a formidable task into manageable steps. Its contribution to timetabling and sequencing the report-writing process will be considered in a moment.

The format I have proposed is simply one of many possibilities. It is important to know at an early stage if a particular format is favoured by your institution. Whatever its precise structure, a simple map of the shape of the final report is essential. There is, however, something contradictory between the static nature of a format and the flow and unpredictability of a journey. See any format as being a useful rather than a constraining device – one that will inevitably require improvisation.

HAVING A TIMETABLE IN MIND:
A ROUTE TOWARDS THE FINAL REPORT

Research projects and research reports have a habit of escaping from the timetables put in place to manage them. Though the practical part of research projects may be completed within a reasonable time frame, the writing of the final research report often seems never-ending.

The format described above not only provides a sketch map of what a research report might look like, it can also serve as a form of timetable for the entire research process. Here I want to address this second function: providing a *chronological sequence* for the writing process.

In the first place, the format prescribes four major steps: *design, implementation, review of process* and *analysis*. This is the key sequence. Within each of these, it suggests a sequence of smaller steps, which peter out when it comes to analysis. I want to argue that the chronology of this four-stage sequence should be scrupulously respected: that the planning and design section should be completed before the review of research implementation and the data summary. And only then should the final analytical chapter be written.

The point of this recommendation is to respect the psychological advantage of writing in 'real time' and avoid the confusion of dabbling with each stage simultaneously. The completion of each stage should provide the foundation for tackling the next. The same principle applies to the steps within each major stage.

The key thing about the 'real time' principle is that each section should be complete, or very close to complete, before the commencement of the next. Each section learns from the previous one and builds reflexively upon it, recognising and addressing its limits. Cosmetic rewriting in hindsight in order to achieve seamless consistency is to be avoided. This encourages a process of endless revision. (The notion of research in 'real time' is discussed in some detail in Appendix 2.)

SUMMARY OF KEY POINTS

* Start with a format in mind for your final report.

* Ensure you understand the four stages of the research report.

* The four stages can provide both a format and a timetable/chronological writing sequence.

* Adhere to the 'real time' principle.

3   Where to start: with theory or practice?

There is nothing so practical as a good theory.

Kurt Lewin (1951, p 169)

INTRODUCTION

We can start classroom research with either a theoretical interest or a practical problem. There are advantages and disadvantages to both. I have chosen to argue for starting with theory. More precisely, I have argued for finding a theoretical way into a practical problem. I think the advantages of doing this outweigh the disadvantages. To illustrate my argument, I shall draw on actual examples of student research that begin with a theoretical idea and move from there into practice.

The argument follows the following sequence of topics:

- what it means to start with 'theory';
- analysing examples of working from theory to practice;
- principles and guidelines.

HOW DO YOU START WITH THEORY?

By 'theory' I do not mean mastery of an established discipline. I am not assuming you have necessarily acquired an adequate grasp of an established intellectual tradition, such as psychology or anthropology or linguistics. My assumption, rather, is that your primary concern is with the practice of becoming an effective classroom teacher. But my second assumption is that prioritising practice does not preclude an interest in theoretical ideas, if these are mediated appropriately.

The way into theory in this limited sense is through some form of *focus*. Focus could be achieved by a theme, an interest or, possibly, the beginnings of a research question. The student research group I wish to discuss began with a common theme, one they soon developed into a useful opening question.

Their theme – emerging from a major interest in their professional teacher education programme – was *narrative or storytelling*. They were interested in how storytelling penetrated into teaching, learning and classroom life. Because they were training to become

Waldorf teachers, they were particularly interested in Waldorf classrooms, with their rich storytelling tradition. Indeed, this group of student researchers had extensive experience of stories and storytelling.

Their research theme was not, however, about the practical skills of telling stories (important as these are) but about something more general and pervasive: how the narrative form seeped into and possibly structured classroom interaction. This was primarily a theoretical concern – and for the more practically minded students, an elusive one to begin with.

Their first step was to *read*, intensively. They were exposed to three stimulating and accessible writers on the nature, power and pervasiveness of the narrative form – Jerome Bruner, Jonathan Gottschall and Kieran Egan. Their influence is apparent in the examples that follow. The crucial thing was that these readings introduced them to exciting theoretical concepts that could be used as lenses through which they could devise their research questions and explore their classrooms. But not all students found it easy to use theory in this way.

Examples of working from theory to practice

The following are brief extracts from seven student researchers' reports on their early attempts to sharpen the focus of their investigation and define their research question. The first four emerging questions make use of some idea or concept discovered in their preliminary reading; the final three do not.

Example 1: Kathy's emerging research question

Phrased differently, my research question then became: 'How is narrative methodology used to connect the known and the unknown in a Waldorf main lesson?' In the classroom the characters can be seen as the children and the teacher; the predicament and the solution will be developed and then solved by those in the classroom. The predicament and the solution will be moulded by the teacher as she will be introducing the content. The teacher will bring to the classroom the information that she has selected to present to the children and she will choose the method to convey this new information. The teacher may choose to take a more back-seat approach, where the children question and discover the content themselves and form their own understanding, or she may prefer to be the driver, feeding children the information. With all of this in mind I have refined my research question in the following way: 'How are narrative predicaments created by the teacher and how do the children engage with them?'

Kathy has found her sharp theoretical focus and her research question in what Gottschall sees as the 'universal grammar' of narrative: '*Story* = *Character* + *Predicament* +

Attempted Extrication' (Gottschall, 2012, p 52). She has discovered an exciting idea: that 'predicament' (some problem that seems impossible to solve) may be as essential for learning and teaching as it is for storytelling. And it is this idea that provides her work with its initial focus, curiosity and intellectual energy.

Example 2: Amy's emerging research question

Clearly I need to find a sharper focus and now I think that my key question will be: 'How does the teacher transform curriculum content into "pedagogical knowledge"?' I want to know how the teacher takes curriculum content and transforms this content in such a way that it becomes meaningful and suitable for the children.

Amy's theoretical discovery is Gudmundsdottir's concept of 'pedagogical knowledge' (Gudmundsdottir, 1995). She wants to understand the rules and procedures whereby formal course descriptions are brought to pedagogic life in the classroom. Her interesting new idea is that every teacher is involved daily – and minute by minute – in an act of 'translation'. She has to translate the abstract ideas and inert information of course requirements into 'pedagogical knowledge' – a form of mediated knowledge that engages hearts and minds in her classroom. She wants to understand the principles involved in this transformation process. Again, this is a highly theoretical question but one that generates real curiosity about daily classroom practice.

Example 3: Christopher's emerging research question

While revisiting Egan's work I was particularly interested in the use of 'binary opposites' and 'affective meaning' as criteria for creating and constructing an effective lesson in which the child can build meaning, and understand the new concepts being brought forward by the teacher. Suddenly my research report began to change shape and direction. It evolved as I suspected it might, and I spent far more time reading Egan's book, 'Teaching as Story Telling'. This further reading led me to my question: 'How do binary opposites facilitate affective meaning and conceptual understanding in this classroom?'

Christopher has found Kieran Egan's argument intriguing: that the resolution of value conflicts in the form of what he calls 'binary opposites' is fundamental both to the story form and to moral, emotional and intellectual engagement in the school curriculum (Egan, 1986). He wants to spend his time in the classroom exploring how teacher and pupils engage with the value choices implicit in a small part of their social studies curriculum.

Example 4: Fay's emerging research question

My interest spiked when Egan suggested that we should not work from the 'known to the unknown' but rather, when content is introduced through the narrative or the story we constantly swing between the 'known and the unknown'. This 'pendulum effect' cannot be physically seen, because it is a swinging process that takes place within our imagination while we listen to story.

Egan writes about the prior knowledge of the child, which he refers to as being 'abstract concepts' that the child already has when entering the schooling system. His theory is that children have the ability to know and understand new tasks and ideas by drawing intuitively on these 'known' abstract concepts.

The above theory led me to my root question: How does the unknown draw out the known within the child? I look at my question as having endless research possibilities. But the fact that my root question is largely theoretical makes my research journey practically impossible to complete. On the other hand, my research question was so alive to me that I could not bring myself to change my question. At this point, it was vital that I find some way in which to investigate my theory practically. It was not until I had grappled with my probable interview categories that I discovered a possible way in which to look practically at my question. I decided that I would focus on lesson content, story and methodology.

Though Fay's question, like Christopher's, derives from Egan's work on storytelling in education – in particular, his sense of the power of intuitively understood 'abstract concepts' as pre-conditions for learning – she will in due course find Vygotsky useful too. Fay is aware that though her theoretical question has become 'alive' for her, it will not be an easy one to pursue in practical terms in the real classroom world. We shall follow her attempt to do this in the following chapter.

Example 5: Mary's emerging research question

Imagination is clearly something of fundamental importance in a story. I am not only concerned with imagination but how it is utilised in story to create meaning. In my observations I will tentatively look at how the teacher utilises imagination in the story form as a link between content and meaning-making. I will observe to find if imagination is the link or are there other aspects of the 'story form' that are creating a link or are helping the imagination in this process of meaning-making. During my data collection and observations in the classroom, I will pay special attention to how the teacher structures the story around his or her interpretation of the content in an imaginative way.

The focus of my research report, therefore, will be on exploring the teacher's imaginative use of the story form to create new understandings. The research question is 'How does the teacher use the story form in an imaginative way to create meaning and understanding within the child?'

Clearly, common-sense language can generate interesting questions without the help of 'theory'. What Mary wishes to explore is a key relationship: between story and new understandings, via imagination. Her key concepts – *story*, *understanding* and *imagination* – are ones she uses every day. But this is a good question because it focuses on trying to understand an assumed relationship: that somehow the use of story acts as a powerful mediator of new understandings. There is a lurking hypothesis here to be tested.

Example 6: Simon's emerging research question

'How does the Story Form work in this Waldorf classroom?' Once we had arrived at this question and after doing preliminary reading, a few aspects of this question started to stand out for me and led me to want to know more. My interest was sparked when thinking about how imagination could be used or awakened in the classroom using the story form. This led me to question how the teacher could engage the children's imagination through story form and how the teacher uses story form in a lesson that is mainly theoretical, like mathematics, to help the children understand new concepts.

Another key aspect stood out for me. When thinking about story form and how it could be used in a classroom I wondered about the children, how the story form would impact them and their responses. Would the story form awaken their imagination and would the story form evoke any emotions? I am interested in seeing whether children can be shaped by story and the impact that story has on them. When considering all of this, a sub-topic started to emerge and brought everything that I am interested in together. The sub-topic that I will be working with is: 'Exploring children's imaginative engagement with the "story form" in a Waldorf School'.

Simon has not found a clear and useful theoretical concept to focus his research question. Instead, he draws on his classroom experience and common-sense language to shape his question: exploring the relationship between storytelling, imagination and understanding. These are important concerns for him professionally and he may well sharpen the focus of his question as his research develops. At present, however, the main terms of his question are dauntingly vague: 'storytelling', 'imagination' and 'understanding'.

In spite of this, he adds on a second question, which he calls a 'sub-topic'. This is concerned with exploring the children's engagement with the story form. Given the vast scope of his inquiry, he will find it difficult to know what to look for in his classroom research site.

Example 7: Ann's emerging research question

For this research report I am taking the framework, story form, and placing it into the classroom to see what fits into which characteristic. Who are the characters? What roles are they playing in this story? What is their problem? What journey are they going on? Where are they starting and where are they going to end? I want to understand the different ways the teacher brings across the content in order for children with different learning difficulties and learning styles to understand. Does she change the way she explains the content so that different children can understand? I also want to look into the way the teacher keeps the children engaged in the content. Does she keep them immersed in what she is teaching by having something to solve or investigate? Or do the children feel the need to investigate further? I am also interested in the way different children interpret what they are being taught. Is there any evidence that some children understand or have better abstract concepts about the content? Does it show in their work?

Ann's attempt is similar to Simon's, in that she makes no use of theoretical concepts discovered in her reading. All her thoughts about a possible research question flow from her common-sense understanding of teaching and learning. What is distinctive about Ann's statement, though, is that she has not yet defined a research question. Instead, she has composed a long list of possible questions. All these questions are interesting ones but she has found no way of solving the problems of focus or selection. She is not in a position to begin her research.

BEGINNING WITH THEORY: SOME PRINCIPLES AND GUIDELINES

Focus

It is interesting but not surprising that the research questions that are most sharply focused are the ones shaped by a theoretical concept that is fresh to the researcher: *narrative predicament*, *pedagogical knowledge*, *binary opposites*. What these concepts have done is provide powerful 'sensitising concepts', conceptual lenses through which to view and explore the situation under study (Blumer, 1954).

Intellectual energy

Nor is it surprising that the discovery of an interesting theoretical focus should generate intellectual energy. Suddenly, a way into a baffling and complex social situation has become available. You are no longer restricted to your own common-sense world. And you are not embarked on a lonely, self-referential journey. You are part of a bigger project.

Intellectual frameworks

Starting with theory provides an intellectual framework for an investigation that is recognisable and accessible to a wide academic readership. Research is being conducted within some form of tradition; it is not idiosyncratic. In the cases discussed above, all researchers are clearly working within the broad framework of 'narrative theory'. Nonetheless, though students have drawn for the most part on the same key texts, they have done so in entirely different ways. They have found different sensitising concepts and have devised different research questions.

Improving practice

Theoretical questions don't preclude practical outcomes. All of the above examples of theoretical questions have practical implications for learning and teaching; and all their writers are concerned with improving their own professional practice. Furthermore, a theoretical starting point by no means displaces, or undervalues, practical, common-sense reasoning. What it does is introduce a fresh stance from which to conduct an inquiry that will inevitably draw on an intuitively understood and accepted body of professional knowledge.

Having a hunch

Perhaps the key advantage of a theory-based question is that it rests on some kind of hunch, some hypothesis, however tentative. This is what distinguishes it from what I have called a 'common-sense' question, one that introduces no fresh terms into everyday language that might disturb taken-for-granted expectations. It is the introduction of a fresh perspective on common-sense practice that provides the provocation that sets the intellectual inquiry in motion.

How long?

How long does it take to move from a (general) research theme to a (specific) research question? In the case of the examples above, it took about two months between the first reading of what became key theoretical texts and the ownership of an individual research question.

SUMMARY OF KEY POINTS

• Identify your theme and establish a focus.

• Read the work of key writers to find a theoretical way into a practical problem.

• Starting with theory provides a recognisable intellectual framework for your investigation.

• You will gradually be able to move from a general research theme to a specific research question.

4 Asking the research question

Experienced researchers discuss their practice of writing notes to themselves as an integral part of the research process.

Pamela Maykut and Richard Morehouse (1994, p 68)

INTRODUCTION

Having a good research question is crucial to the success of any research inquiry. This chapter:

- defines criteria that a good research question should meet;
- applies these criteria to six examples of research questions;
- proposes general guidelines for asking good questions.

WHAT COUNTS AS A GOOD RESEARCH QUESTION?

Arguably, the most important step in the entire research process is asking the 'right' research question. *But what counts as a good research question?* Let's examine the six answers below, and then apply these criteria to examples of research questions.

WHAT IS A GOOD RESEARCH QUESTION?

1. One we don't know the answer to.
2. One that is theoretically framed and interesting – it has 'energy'.
3. One that is short, sweet and sharply focused.
4. One that generates other questions.
5. One that has practical and personal value.
6. One that is 'doable' (answerable) in the time and under the conditions available.

1. One that we don't know the answer to

A surprising number of research questions are able to generate predictable answers. This may lead to the worst possible research scenario – where the researcher knows in advance what the research findings will be but is obliged to pretend ignorance. This is a recipe for dummy research. By contrast, a genuine uncertainty and curiosity about where the question will lead is what generates intellectual energy.

2. One that is theoretically framed and interesting – it has 'energy'

This is the kind of question I have argued for – and provided examples of – in the previous chapter.

3. One that is short, sweet and sharply focused

Many research questions are in fact several questions, or contain the ghosts of earlier questions that have escaped exorcism. The complexities (and even contradictions) of multiple questions emerge when they are put to practical use in classroom observation. And even more research questions turn out to be too vague to provide the focus that classroom observation and interview require.

4. One that generates other questions

A good research question leads to further questions. It starts a chain of inquiry. We will examine this generative process in practice in Chapters 5 and 6.

5. One that has practical and personal value

Both professional and personal development are important expectations of classroom research, and it is important that student researchers attempt to clarify the practical skills or strategies they might develop as by-products of their investigation, as well as benefits of a more personal kind that immersion in the research process might offer.

6. One that is 'doable' (answerable) in the time and under the conditions available

This is a key criterion, and is closely related to the issue of sharp focus. Most research questions are, in their early forms, vague, general and hugely ambitious. If they remain so, trying to answer them will be a demoralising experience.

EXAMINING EXAMPLES OF RESEARCH QUESTIONS

You have encountered the following six research questions before, but they are now in a revised and shortened form. To what extent do these questions meet the criteria discussed above?

> 1. *Kathy: How are narrative predicaments created by the teacher and how do the children engage with them?*

The question is sharply focused on 'narrative predicaments', but a possible problem is that there are two questions here. However, the first question both leads to and actually requires the second for the concept of 'narrative predicament' to be understood in practical terms. It requires both teacher and children to create a 'predicament'.

Kathy can have no idea of the actual examples of narrative predicament she will encounter in her research site and of how these will be generated. She does not know the answer to her question and for this reason it can be said to hold intellectual energy. Certainly, the question can be seen as leading to fresh insights into motivation and intellectual growth, and will benefit her professional development. And it has a good chance of being answered under the conditions she faces.

> 2. *Amy: How does the teacher transform content knowledge into 'pedagogical knowledge' in order to engage the children's imagination?*

The focus of this question is on the conversion of one form of knowledge into another. The question is interesting, short and sweet, and neatly defined, but it is far from simple. It contains, in effect, two interrelated questions: how does this conversion process actually take place; and how does the new form of knowledge produced actually engage the children's imagination?

A possible problem in pursuing this question lies in the two key terms 'pedagogical knowledge' and 'imagination'. Both are vast and imprecise concepts and problems of clarity and focus lie ahead. This may have a bearing on the first criterion: *one we don't know the answer to.* The researcher may well find her common-sense expectations of good pedagogy and imaginative involvement confirmed in her research classroom. She may lose the explanatory power of the 'how' questions and find herself simply describing 'good practice'. But this may not happen. Certainly, the question begins as an exciting and potentially open-ended one.

> 3. *Christopher: How do binary opposites facilitate affective meaning and conceptual understanding in this classroom?*

This is another theoretically framed 'how' question that explores a *relationship* and one that he would certainly not be able to answer in advance. The question has a sharp focus: on 'binary opposites', a concept that has been clearly defined for him by Kieran Egan. He will need to identify such binary opposites at work in classroom discourse over a period of time. And he will then have to explore how these value oppositions have (or have not) engaged learners' feelings and stimulated their conceptual development. This latter step will not be an easy task: both feelings and conceptual development may prove difficult to perceive and identify. But this is a stimulating project and one that will hold practical and professional insights for the researcher.

> 4. *Fay: How does the unknown draw out the known within the child?*

As she has pointed out, this daunting question fascinates Fay. She sees it as having practical and personal value. Though she realises how difficult it will be to pursue it in practice, she is determined to stick with it. What she finds intriguing, and what gives the question its energy, is the theory that some intuitive sense of 'the unknown' may be a precondition for jumps in conceptual understanding. She wants to explore this possibility. Her key difficulty will be grasping the 'the unknown'; grasping 'the known' may turn out to be difficult too.

> 5. *Mary: How does the teacher use the story form in an imaginative way to create meaning and understanding within the child?*

Mary wants to explore a relationship: how imaginative use of narrative facilitates conceptual development. This is a question that has practical and personal value. The question is short and terse but it is not clearly focused; and it is defined in common-sense terms that are not sharpened or probed in any way. It is possible that given her teaching experience, she will have firm ideas and expectations about the nature of this relationship, and the consequence of this may be that in pursuing her question she will fall back on her common-sense understandings of what constitutes good practice. But this may not happen. The relationship she wishes to explore is an interesting and important one and her work may well generate fresh insights.

> 6. *Simon: How can the teacher engage the children's imagination through the story form and how does the teacher use the story form in a lesson that is mainly theoretical, like mathematics, to help the children understand new concepts?*

Simon's question is very similar to Mary's, in three ways. It is personally and professionally important; it is interested in exploring the relationship between imaginative use of the story form and conceptual development; and it too is framed in common-sense language, appropriating no new concepts to shape a theoretical focus.

However, there are two vast interrelated questions here, not one: how is imagination engaged, and how do abstract concepts come to be understood? The obvious problem, therefore, is one of *focus*. A choice has to be made if the research task is to be 'doable'. Without a much sharper focus it will be difficult for Simon to know what to look for in the classroom world. Under such conditions, he too may be tempted to fall back on an exposition of good practice in answer to his question. But, again, this may not be the case. Qualitative research takes unpredictable turns.

7. *Ann: (No research question defined)*

Ann remained unable to decide on her research question. She entered her classroom with only the list of interests reported on in the last chapter. Gradually, a very broad research focus emerged during the observation and interview process.

SOME GENERAL GUIDELINES

Cognitive level of questions

Many beginner researchers find it difficult to define their research question. Some are not used to asking questions that do not ask for information, and have little grasp of the range of intellectual tasks that questions challenge us to explore. Bloom's Taxonomy is useful in providing striking insight into the cognitive range of questions available to the researcher (Bloom et al, 1956).

'How' questions

All of the questions we have examined are 'how' questions. They want to know how important things happen in the classroom. But there are 'how' questions and 'How' questions. A 'how' question may turn out to be a disguised 'what' question. I argued that there was a risk of this happening to Mary's and Simon's questions.

Tweaking the research question

No research question is fully understood at the time of asking. When it is used as an exploratory tool in a real situation it reveals its tricky and stubborn qualities. And these need to be engaged with for as long as possible. However, few research questions survive entirely intact. Most are changed or tweaked during the research process, in particular during the data collection stage. It is important that researchers recognise and report such changes.

Dummy questions

None of the above questions can be labelled 'dummy' questions but one or two, as I have argued, may deliver predictable results. All the above questions could be answerable in the time available, given a realistic plan of action. We examine such plans of action in the next chapter.

SUMMARY OF KEY POINTS

Generate a 'good' research question by interrogating it thoroughly against each of the six criteria listed at the start of this chapter.

Putting the research question to work Part 1: developing observation guides

As much as possible the researcher tries to capture people's exact words in the field notes.

Pamela Maykut and Richard Morehouse (1994, p 76)

INTRODUCTION

This chapter looks at the ways in which research questions are put to work. We follow the fortunes of two research questions, asked by Kathy and Fay, as they are used to explore two very different classrooms. They have been chosen for four reasons:

1. The questions are promising ones.
2. They require different approaches.
3. They encountered difficulties.
4. In due course they generated excellent research reports.

For each research question example I will:

- examine how the observation guide was developed;
- explore how the guide fared in practice in the classroom;
- assess its strengths and weaknesses;
- draw out some general conclusions about the use of observation guides.

PUTTING KATHY'S RESEARCH QUESTION TO WORK

Kathy worked long and hard to find a clear and simple theoretical research focus. The result is a terse and neatly focused research question: *How are narrative predicaments created by the teacher and how do the children engage with them?*

Her task now is to put this question to work in practice. She needs to clarify what things she might concentrate on, during classroom observation and in interviews. She may need to distinguish between what she is looking *for* and what she should be looking *at*. The thinking process she will go through begins with her research question and takes fairly logical steps through asking and answering the following questions:

1. What is my theoretical focus? *Narrative predicaments.*
2. What am I looking *for? Examples of 'narrative predicaments'.*
3. What do I want to discover? *What forms these predicaments take. How they work. How children engage with them.* These questions shape her *observation categories.*
4. To discover this, what do I need to look *at*? What practical things do I need to pay attention to?
   Answers to these questions shape her *observation guide*. This might include *tasks, questions, problems and difficulties.*

Kathy's observation guide (first stage)

The following is Kathy's report on how she actually constructed her observation guide.

> *To record and collect data I will use two approaches: field notes and a research journal. The research journal I will use for the jotting down of notes and other personal comments on what is happening in the classroom. The field notes, however, keep a more objective and unbiased account of what happened such as recording the exact words said in the classroom.*

Research journal example:

Predicament number, date and time	Characters involved	Predicament	Children's reactions	Solution
1				
2				
3				

Field notes example:

Predicament number, date and time	Exact words of teacher	Body language of teacher	Exact words of student A	The body language of student A	Personal reflection on predicament
1					
2					
3					

The two main observation categories that I will be focusing on, while in the classroom, will be: narrative predicaments and how the children engage with them. I am not sure exactly what it is that I will be able to observe so I have tentatively constructed a framework to work around.

Narrative predicament:

* *What problem/problems have arisen?*

* *What caused the problem?*

* *Was it part of the teacher's design?*

* *At what stage of the lesson did it surface?*

Children's engagement:

* *How did the children react to the predicaments?*

* *How was this reaction translated into their workbooks?*

Kathy's observation guide (second stage)

Before entering the classroom Kathy had not realised how demanding and difficult it would be to use such a detailed and systematic guide in a complex, dynamic and unpredictable situation. But after a very short time in the classroom she abandoned her original guide and reports as follows:

It did not take long for me to abandon my original observation guidelines described in chapter one. I felt that I was looking for too much information and I was becoming too involved in trying to record it, causing me to become too detached from what was going on in the classroom. By day two I had created a new set of observation guidelines that were slightly simpler:

Daily observation

Rhythmic time (the first section of the lesson dominated by movement)

No.	Time	Activity description	Predicament	Quote (relevant quote to help back up any future findings)	Thought (personal perception of the situation)
1					
2					
3					
4					

Main lesson

No.	Time	Activity description	Predicament	Quote	Thought
1					
2					
3					
4					

Kathy's observation guide (third stage)

Kathy's revised guide lasted only a day. It too proved too restrictive. She reports on the third and final stage – a simple, workable and intuitively satisfying solution – as follows.

However, by the end of day three I had abandoned this too. I was limiting myself too much with these structured tables. I needed to be able to record my data more freely. In the end I found the best approach to be writing down the process of the lesson and highlighting:

* *predicament (in blue);*

* *pure observation, describing exactly what was happening in the classroom without any of my own personal bias (in pink);*

* *personal thoughts (in yellow).*

At the end of the day I would sort the data into the above mentioned categories.

The process I used helped me to see clearly the difference between what I had actually observed and what I had thought.

Discussion: Kathy's observation guide in practice

Getting in the way

The swift, progressive and surgical simplification of Kathy's observation guides when tested in practice is exemplary. Obviously, they are getting in the way: they are far too restrictive. More precisely, they are preventing an intelligent and empathetic grasp of what is going on in the classroom, as well as an intelligent quest for deepening an understanding of and answering her research question. And this is because they are fragmenting what needs to be understood as a whole and over a period of time. They are turning Kathy into a *classifier*.

Reflexivity

What is exemplary, too, about her ruthless treatment of her observation guides is her capacity for reflexivity – for looking back from a fresh vantage point (in this case only a day later), making a diagnosis, however intuitive, of a problem experienced, and acting on this diagnosis.

What Kathy is doing is learning in 'real time' – taking stock of a situation, seeing things in a new way, and acting on this new perception to change her strategy. In her report she does not disguise or omit earlier understandings; she recognises and reports on them as steps in her research journey.

PUTTING FAY'S RESEARCH QUESTION TO WORK

Fay's observation guide

Fay's research question is: *How does the unknown draw out the known within the child?* She outlines her sense of the major steps that lie ahead of her and she explains her design of an observation guide.

> *Firstly, I must establish what subject will be taught and if possible what topic within the subject will be taught, for example, punctuation in English. My next step would be to look at how the teacher uses the imaginative story or the imaginative experience to introduce the new content. I will also pay specific attention to the plot of the story and at which point within the story the academic content is first introduced. Then, once I have established that, I will focus on the method that the teacher uses to integrate the academic content with the imaginative content without straying too far from reality, the balance between the reality and the imagination.*
>
> *My hope for investigating my research question in this way is that by observing the class and the teacher for two weeks, I will find a loophole in which I can crack the theoretical code and find an answer to my question.*

THE OBSERVATION GUIDE

I have chosen to use my probable interview categories as my tentative observation categories as well. I feel that what I may be observing in the classroom will be different to the answers that I will get from the interviewee. Also, I may have missed something in my observation that the teacher will mention during the interview. My interview will mostly be focusing on the work of the teacher, whereas my observation will largely be focusing on the child and how he reacts to certain information. My tentative observation categories include the following:

- **The academic content being taught:**

Here I will observe the subject being taught. Specific focus will be given to the topic within the subject being taught, for example, fractions within maths.

- **Skills/abilities (known and unknown):**

When observing this I will look at prior (known) skills/abilities of the children before new content is taught. This will be observed when the teacher does recall.

I will use the follow-up activity to identify the new skills/abilities (unknown) that the children learnt from the new content that was taught.

- **Story/working with the imagination:**

I will be observing how the teacher incorporates imagination into the lesson through experience or story.

How imagination is used to introduce the content.

How is the imagination connected to the subject content?

- **Methodology:**

I will also be looking at the plot of the story and at which point in the story the teacher first introduces the subject content.

How the teacher uses imagination to make sense of the subject content.

- **Working with the new skills and abilities:**

I want to observe what methods the teacher uses to work with the story content that was told.

How is this new content consolidated?

I will be recording my data through the use of field notes.

Fay's observation guide in practice

Fay reports on her experience of using her observation guide as follows:

THE ACTUAL OBSERVATION PROCESS

I mentioned that I would be making use of field notes. Initially, I went into the classroom with the intention to always continue with this way of recording my data. However, halfway through the first main lesson I started feeling restricted, as if the use of field notes was only allowing me to record limited data when I needed to record so much more. I switched to a day by day recording method where I was able to record everything of relevance, in my opinion. However, at one point, during my second day of observation, I completely misjudged the relevance of information being given to the children and ended up needing to go back the next day to try and record that information. This information was the highlight of my data collection. I will fully elaborate on this in my section 2.2.

My observation categories were supposed to be my pillar on which to lean. But instead, they ended up being more of a stem that I was able to bend. The reason for saying the above is that initially I intended to organise my data every day and fit my data under the correct observation categories. However, soon I realised that even though I would, while observing, identify a category for that data, not all the categories could be seen every day. This made me feel quite scattered. By the end of my third day in the class, I took the decision not to use my categories for the rest of my time at the school.

My observation categories were the points that buckled under pressure. Initially, these helped me to get started on my observations, but in the end, they were the categories that I decided not to use until the end of my research period. My observation categories became too restrictive and caused me to be more scattered than structured. Interestingly enough, my observation categories were clearer than my interview categories in my research design.

Discussion

Focusing on interconnection

Fay has developed a systematic and logical preliminary model of what she wants to observe and examine. She has six points of focus that she sees as essential to answering her research question. All these points of focus are *interconnected* and will need to be understood in their dynamic relationship to one another. In other words, her question requires her to understand an aspect of teaching-learning in its totality, as it develops over a period of time.

Blocking insight: scattered not structured

After a very short time in her research classroom Fay does exactly what Kathy has done: she first simplifies and then abandons her observation guide. She diagnoses the problem that led to this decision as follows: *'My observation categories became too restrictive and caused me to be more scattered than structured'*. Her observation guide, like Kathy's, was in fact blocking insight into what was happening in the classroom. The word 'scattered' reveals the nature of this blocking: a classification system was preventing her from seeing things as a whole, and this fragmentation of perception was causing her to lose her grip on the research question that drove her inquiry.

Fragmentation

She gives a vivid example of the nature and consequence of fragmentation. She reports as follows: *'At one point, during my second day of observation, I completely misjudged the relevance of information being given to the children'*. Her misjudgement arose because she had not yet grasped the intellectual and pedagogic flow taking place in her classroom. She understands this flow retrospectively, a day later. Only then is she able to see the significance of this event in providing a key to answering her question.

A radical solution

Her solution to dealing with her observation guide is, like Kathy's, a radical one. She puts it like this: *'I switched to a day by day recording method where I was able to record everything of relevance, in my opinion'*. In other words, she sat in the classroom armed only with her research question and her intuitive, common-sense understanding of how primary school classrooms worked and jotted down whatever she thought might be important.

CLASSROOM OBSERVATION:

SOME GENERAL CONCLUSIONS

Do we need observation guides?

An obvious question arises: do we need observation guides? Is it not sufficient to enter the research classroom armed with a good – and well-understood – research question and do what Fay eventually did: *'record everything of relevance, in my opinion'*. The phrase *in my opinion* is the crucial one. An observation guide must not turn an intelligent, inquiring researcher into a classifier, a collector. The researcher's task is one of ongoing, intelligent interpretation of what is going on, of what may be relevant in the pursuit of answers to her question. In qualitative research, *What is happening here?* remains the fundamental question on which to concentrate.

There is certainly a case for abandoning research guides. There is also a case for rethinking their form and function. The key principles seem to be simplicity and ease of use. They must not get in the way.

Sound recordings

Given the problems with making a detailed record of observations, a good sound recording of classroom interaction becomes important. Fay's retrospective grasp of what she had missed was possible only because she had made a simple sound recording of the previous day's lesson.

Openness and reflexivity

Whatever the strategy used, openness and reflexivity are crucial ingredients of the qualitative researcher's craft. The researcher must be able to be surprised, to learn from his or her surprise and to act on new insights in real time.

A case for observation guides?

Although both of the initial observation guides were abandoned in favour of much simpler and more usable models, the intellectual work involved in their creation was not wasted. They were an important attempt to grasp the practical dimensions of a theoretical problem. And they would be drawn on to inform two key tasks that lay ahead: the organisation of research data (see Chapter 9) and the analysis of this data (see Chapter 10).

SUMMARY OF KEY POINTS

- Your task as a researcher is one of ongoing, intelligent interpretation of what you observe.

- Use sound recording to capture subtle data.

- Creating and then modifying an observation guide is a valuable exercise that will aid understanding of your investigation.

6 Putting the research question to work Part 2: developing interview guides

An interview is a conversation with a purpose.
Pamela Maykut and Richard Morehouse (1994, p 79)

INTRODUCTION

This chapter continues to draw on Kathy and Fay's developing work in order to consider the second major way of putting the research question to use: the devising of interview guides. Classroom research generally requires teacher interviews in addition to observation. These two sources of data both complement and have an interrogatory relationship with each other. In particular, interviews allow researchers to explore the teacher's interpretation of classroom events, which may challenge his or her own understandings. The chapter:

*   examines how both Kathy and Fay developed their interview guides;
*   reports on how these guides fared in practice in the classroom;
*   discusses their strengths and limitations;
*   draws some general conclusions.

KATHY'S INTERVIEW GUIDE

Kathy explains the development of her interview guide as follows. It could not be more different from her highly detailed and systematic original observation guide. She wants to ensure that she covers three broad categories of inquiry. Her actual questions will be left to shape themselves in the moment and as part of a conversation.

> An interview guide cannot be left too open otherwise the interview may stray too far away from the main points of interest. As I am easily led astray by my own thoughts my guide will not be made up of broad questions but rather a list of categories of enquiry. In my case these will be very similar to my observation categories: 'character', 'problem', 'solution'.

> *For example, after explaining my interests in some detail to the teacher I might ask:*
>
> *Narrative predicament: 'What is your preferred method of encouraging the children to engage with the lesson (movement, stories, etc)?'*
>
> *'Do you ever intentionally cause a predicament (or problem, or puzzle, etc) in the classroom and if so, in what format?'*
>
> *Class engagement: 'In what ways does your class react to a challenge?'*

Kathy's interview guide in practice

Kathy reported on the actual use of her interview guide as follows:

> *I had hoped that my initial meeting with my host teacher, before the observation period, would be a short and informal 'meet and greet'; however, it turned into a full interview. Her passion for her class and for the theme I would be working with shone through clearly. She was already familiar with the Gottschall article that I had chosen to focus on. Her understanding of what I would be looking for led to a much more insightful interview than I had expected. We quickly leapt into deep water as she grappled with my topic and the possible ways I could go about interpreting it.*
>
> *After a few days of observation I approached my host teacher to request a formal interview on the Friday. I followed the same procedure the following week. The two Friday interviews allowed the teacher and me to reflect on the week together. For both interviews I introduced a topic that had stood out for me that week and we held an informal discussion on that subject.*
>
> *This approach varied from what I had identified in chapter one as my ideal interview; however, I felt that since both my teacher and I had a firm grasp of what I was trying to observe I did not need to limit myself with a list of categories to structure discussion.*
>
> *My host teacher was always available for more impromptu meetings at the end of each lesson if I requested any clarification of something I had observed.*

Discussion

The teacher as co-researcher

Once again, a pre-prepared guide – even as open a one as this – has been abandoned. And for good reason. Kathy's class teacher did not wish to be interviewed; she wanted a *discussion*. This was her classroom, these were her children, she understood narrative theory and the unfolding lesson was her creation. She clearly saw herself as a co-thinker if not a co-researcher. And she proved an insightful and articulate theorist of her own practice. Kathy was very fortunate.

The interview as conversation

One of the ideals of good interviewing is to enable focused *conversation*. In this case, conversation was demanded. Under such circumstances, all an interview guide could become was, at most, a very general checklist. Kathy's brief and almost casual guide turned out to be perfect for the situation. Something more detailed and prescriptive could have stifled the range and depth of conversation.

Engaging two sources of data

The two formally arranged end-of-week meetings began in a way that could only have been planned a day or two in advance. Kathy began by introducing a topic that had stood out for her during her observation, and the interview began with an informal discussion on that subject. In this way Kathy's two sources of data engaged with each other. She was able to interrogate and deepen her understanding of her observation data, helped by the teacher's own retrospective reflection.

Rules of engagement

Note that the class teacher wanted to know in advance what Kathy's research was about. She wanted to engage with it theoretically, from start to finish. This case provides a powerful answer to the question of how much briefing on the research project should be shared with the interviewee. This class teacher wanted total disclosure and she received it. But not all teachers will wish for or relish such intellectual and personal investment. Kathy was wise and confident enough to accept these unexpected rules of engagement – not that she had much choice.

FAY'S INTERVIEW GUIDE

Fay explains as follows how she went about designing her interview guide.

I regard an interview as being a prepared conversation with set questions designed to purposely collect evidence concerning a certain topic.

A good interview consists of questions that are open-ended, questions that require more than a yes or no answer. A good interview should also rest on trust that has built up between the interviewer and the interviewee.

My interview questions will be set up in a particular sequence. These questions will move from practical to more theoretical, from simple to more complex, as the investigation goes on. One thing that I constantly ask myself while devising interview questions is: will I learn something from these questions and how is it relevant to my investigation?

There are different ways in which to conduct an interview, but I will make use of an interview guide. An interview guide allows me to come up with a very precise list of broad questions that will allow me to explore my research question and probe the interviewee for answers. It has few restrictions and does not confine me to one topic alone.

When planning interviews in this way, I need to create interview categories that will make it easier to group similar themes and ideas together. I have created these categories in a way that will allow me to gain insight into my research question.

Interview categories:

My research question consists of five possible interview categories:

- *academic content (subject content that is being taught);*

- *skills/abilities (known and unknown): for research purposes:*

  - *known = prior skills and abilities that children have when coming from the previous grade;*
  - *unknown = skills and abilities that children will have once the new content has been taught;*

- *story/working with the imagination;*

- *methodology (How is the academic content connected to the story?);*

- *working with the new skills and abilities.*

For each of the above categories I have come up with one or two possible key questions:

- Distinguish what content in a subject is being <u>taught</u>.

- What prior skills/abilities did the children acquire in the previous grade concerning the subject content? (known)

- What new skills/abilities will the children learn from this new content? (unknown)

- How do you as the teacher take the subject content and link it to the children's imagination?

- How do you manage to not lose focus of the essence of the content while still working with the imagination?

- After the children have acquired the new skills and abilities, do you think that these can now be considered as being part of their known knowledge?

  - If yes, what are the first steps used to work with this new-found knowledge?
  - If no, what is the next step towards making it known?

In my follow-up interview I would like to include questions derived from things that I have observed.

Fay's interview guide in practice

This is a far more detailed and systematic interview guide than Kathy's. It contains not only key categories in logical sequence derived from her research question but precisely defined questions within each category. Surprisingly, given Kathy's experience, she experienced no difficulty in using it in practice. She reported as follows:

THE INTERVIEWING PROCESS

I decided to follow the interview plans that I included in my research design. I was lucky enough to have my teacher agree to two interviews, one at the end of each week.

My first interview consisted of my key questions under each category in my research design and one or two questions that developed from answers given by the teacher. I truly believed that these questions would give me better insight into the teacher's way of teaching and the children's level of understanding. At this point in my research this was my main focus.

My second interview was on my final day in the classroom. These interview questions were drawn up based on things that I observed and things that could possibly happen after I leave.

I never felt the need or urgency to ask the teacher a question related to my research any other time besides during my interviews. If ever there was a question, I would write it down in my journal and preserve it for my interview. This was my method of ensuring that I did not miss out on any opportunities to record important information.

In the very first conversation with my teacher, I asked permission to record our interviews on my cellular device. He agreed to this, and all our interviews were recorded in this manner. This gave me an opportunity to really listen to what the teacher was saying and then later go over the recording and analyse the interview. All interviews took place in the staffroom, where no other staff members were present. This was a very serene, safe and comfortable environment for both the participant and for me.

The one definite strength that emerged from my research design was my interview categories and my key questions. Throughout my research, the one section that barely changed was my interview section. When my interview questions were based on my observations, my interview categories clarified my data and helped me put my findings into perspective.

Discussion

Conventional boundaries

Clearly, the relationship between Fay and her class teacher was very different from the one Kathy encountered. Here, conventional boundaries were observed. The teacher's task was to teach and assist the researcher by answering questions, not to intrude on the researcher's role. And the researcher's task was to conduct formal interviews; this was her responsibility. There was no sharing of ownership of the research project, and no evidence of shared theorising. Altogether, this seemed a cooler, more restricted encounter.

Sticking to the guide

The second striking difference is that Fay found her interview guide useful and stuck to it. She puts it like this: *'The one definite strength that emerged from my research design was my interview categories and my key questions'*. This can be explained in part by her formal relationship with the class teacher. He allows her to set the interview agenda; and he responds with answers to her predefined questions. She is in control.

However, it can be explained, too, by the nature of Fay's guide. It is a formidable intellectual summary of an assumed pattern: the pattern of a journey by a learner into the unknown. It is a highly theorised account of what Fay expects and hopes to discover. It has its own authoritative logic. And it was this logic that probably dominated the interview process. There was not a great deal of room for divergence or contestation. We may be able to test this hunch when we examine Fay's summary of her interview data in the following section.

USING INTERVIEW GUIDES:
SOME GENERAL CONCLUSIONS

Unilateral definition

What becomes clear from this comparison is that the classroom researcher cannot unilaterally define the rules for conducting an interview and should not attempt to do so. The contrasting styles and emerging rules of the two interview sequences were constructed by the personalities and expectations of four very different people.

Comfortable forms of conversation

The key thing about both interview sequences was that they worked. Both Kathy and Fay gained a great deal from their interviews, and both were very satisfied with them. Clearly, intentionally or otherwise, they had constructed (or allowed to be constructed) forms of conversation which they found comfortable and productive.

Each interview relationship is unique

It seems important, therefore, to regard each interview relationship as unique, to approach it respectfully and openly, and invite discussion on how best to proceed. Without full and open participation by the teacher in a way in which he or she is comfortable, classroom research is severely limited.

The teacher as co-theorist

Finally, the importance of recognising the teacher as a co-theorist, or at least a potential co-theorist, needs to be stressed. The class teacher holds an intuitive or explicit theory of the work the class is engaged in. They know the children and understand the class dynamics. A huge amount of insight is lost if the teacher keeps what he really thinks to himself.

SUMMARY OF KEY POINTS

- Interview structures and outcomes are fluid and dependent on the individuals taking part.

- Approach your interviews respectfully and openly to maximise their validity and usefulness.

- Embrace your interviewee as a co-theorist and keeper of knowledge.

7   Writing your research plan

Good academic writing is good clear writing. Nothing more and nothing less.
Michael Newman (2014, p 5)

INTRODUCTION

What we have done in the last few chapters is work through the planning and design stage of the research project. We have focused on starting points, defining the research question and putting the question to work through classroom observation and interviews. And we have moved a bit beyond the design stage by examining how the observation and interview guides of two research students have actually survived the reality of the classroom.

This chapter is a form of stock-taking. Before we move to the next key stages in the research process – summarising and analysing the research data – I want to consider how to complete the writing of the first part of the research report, the research plan. To do this, I will make use of the format described in Chapter 2. And once again, I will draw on Kathy and Fay's work.

The proposed research plan consists of seven sections in the following sequence:

1. The research theme.
2. Preliminary reading.
3. The research question.
4. Research approach and methods.
5. Research site.
6. Research ethics.
7. Purposes and expectations.

The more practical and strategic aspects of research design – asking the research question and devising observation and interview guides – have been dealt with in Chapters 4, 5 and 6. Here we will concentrate on the other necessary components of the first stage of the research report.

BEGIN WITH THE RESEARCH THEME

Introducing the research plan with a statement of the research theme signals the theoretical focus of the investigation; it requires the researcher to demonstrate his or her grasp of the theme briefly and clearly; and to indicate why the theme holds interest for him or her as a researcher. It is an opportunity to demonstrate, right from the start, personal ownership of the project at a theoretical level. It sets the tone for what is to come.

This short introduction should include a discussion of the central ideas that might provide a focus for the investigation. And key quotations should be included too. Kathy's research theme was *the work of the story form in a classroom setting*. In her brief introduction she summed up as follows what she saw as a central idea:

> *If stories dominate our everyday learning then surely it should be stories that dominate the schooling system and perhaps they do. We may not be aware of them as they work their magic on a deeper, unseen level. And this is what I would like to explore and understand.*

In presenting what she saw as central ideas, Fay selected quotations that she had found particularly stimulating:

> *'...the human mind was shaped for story, so that it could be shaped by story.'*
>
> (Gottschall, 2012, p 56)
>
> *'The importance of the narrative for the cohesion of a culture is as great, very likely, as it is in structuring an individual life.'*
>
> (Bruner, 1996, p 40)

Both Kathy and Fay presented a brief account of the research theme that brought it to life personally. And both of them had the beginnings of an idea of what they might investigate.

PRELIMINARY READING

I use the term 'preliminary reading' in preference to the term 'review of the literature' for two reasons. Firstly, it indicates the modest and limited scope of this section: no claims are made to review the state of research in a particular field. Secondly, it signals that the selected readings have a preparatory function: helping to focus and define the research question.

The key thing is the intellectual quality, not the quantity, of the papers reviewed. Their task is to offer interesting ways of grasping the research theme: to provide a useful theoretical framework within which to work towards the research question.

There are two main ways of organising the review of readings. The more sophisticated way is to do this topic by topic, or idea by idea. In this way, the ideas of individual writers may be discussed and compared. The more common and simpler approach, especially when texts are being explored for the first time, is to proceed writer by writer. This is what Kathy and Fay have done. However, they have enriched this approach by commenting on parallels and connections. The advantage of proceeding writer by writer is the sense of personal discovery that is communicated.

We shall examine Kathy's and Fay's handling of the preliminary reading section below.

Kathy's preliminary reading section

Kathy has discovered five writers of importance to her. She discusses their central ideas on the role of storytelling in our lives and in education in particular; and she explores the ways in which their ideas interrelate and complement one another. She finds the work of Gottschall and Bruner particularly stimulating:

The first extracts that I dived into were those from the book 'The Storytelling Animal: How Stories Make Us Human' by Jonathan Gottschall. The effect these readings had on me was profound. They entirely shifted my thoughts and feelings on what I thought lay ahead. The word 'story' took on new meaning. My new-found concept was that story permeates every part of my life and holds truly monumental importance in our everyday lives. This revelation is that we as humans, and the society that we live in, could not exist if it were not for the power of stories, 'humans are creatures of story, so story touches nearly every aspect of our lives' (Gottschall, 2012, p 15).

Bruner talks more simply of there always needing to be trouble in a story to make it appealing, 'At a minimum, a "story" (fictional or actual) involves an Agent who Acts to achieve a Goal in a recognisable Setting by the use of certain Means. What drives the story, what makes it worth telling is Trouble...' (Bruner, 1996, p 94). Both agree that without 'trouble' or some sort of 'predicament' the story will not be appealing to its listeners – would not be a 'story'.

It will be the second of these insights that will in due course direct her research focus and her research question. As we have seen, the idea of 'narrative predicament' will become her central interest.

Fay's preliminary reading section

Fay surveys eight theorists of narrative. Some are general theorists and others are concerned with learning and teaching. What she finds of particular interest is the crucial place of imagination in storytelling:

> *Going through my readings I searched for answers as to what this dimension could be. What can be so powerful that it can transport your mind from one place to another? I came to a one-word conclusion, imagination. Gottschall (2012, p 144) writes about 'ink people' and how they are nothing but 'wiggles of ink on paper'. It is imagination that breathes life into them. Without imagination stories would cease to exist.*

She finds Gudmundsdottir's ideas stimulating, particularly those to do with the role of imagination in conceptual development and her idea that the teacher needs *'pedagogically-seeking-eyes'*.

> *'The texts used in teaching, such as textbooks and other curriculum material, require that teachers look at them with "pedagogically-seeking-eyes"' (Gudmundsdottir, 1995, p 32). What I infer from the term 'pedagogically-seeking-eyes' is that teachers need to look at the resources made available to them and ask themselves how the content can be brought to life.*

Finally, she notes an intriguing idea in Egan's work. He dismisses the maxim that teaching should move from the concrete to the abstract, and stresses the importance in learning of children's intuitive abstract knowledge. Fay sums this up as follows:

> *Egan (1989) goes further to say that any knowledge can be introduced to a child as long as it can engage with their 'abstract conceptual' ability. He also makes the point that children may not have the concept of logic but they have the abstract abilities to move a story forward.*

Fay will make use of all these ideas, especially Egan's, in discovering her own research focus: exploring the process of swinging between the known and the unknown in the learning process.

RESEARCH APPROACH AND METHODS

What the researcher has to do here is demonstrate the fit between research question and the choice of research methods. And how such methods will be implemented needs to be discussed in practical terms.

Methods are not simply technical matters; they form part of a set of theoretical assumptions about what counts as research. I have advocated a qualitative research approach, and I would expect students to explain what this means before introducing and justifying specific methods.

Step 1

Their first task, then, would be to give a brief account of qualitative research and explain why it is appropriate for investigating what is going on in classrooms. I have provided a sketch of a possible argument in Chapter 3.

Step 2

Their second task would be to examine the research question and ask how it might be answered. What kinds of data would be required to answer it and how might this data be collected and recorded?

Step 3

Their third task would be to discuss the two methods particularly appropriate for qualitative classroom research – observation and interview.

Observation

Kathy describes her intended approach to observation as follows:

As I will be observing the class there is no other choice but for me to be in the classroom, watching. I will attempt to interfere with the class as little as possible. The main objective is to remain unnoticed and avoid causing any alterations to the lesson being taught.

To record and collect data I will use two approaches: field notes and a research journal. The research journal I will use for the jotting down of notes and other personal comments on what is happening in the classroom. The field notes, however, keep a more objective and unbiased account of what happened such as recording the exact words said in the classroom.

Fay introduces this task in a particularly frank way:

> *I will have my root research question from which sub-questions will arise as my investigation goes on. I have no clue what will happen when I enter the classroom. I intend to observe particular things that might be happening when content is taught and how this process affects the participants.*

But she then proceeds to show that she has very clear ideas about the form her observation and interviews might take.

Interviewing

Fay describes the approach she will take for interviewing as follows:

> *I will ask the teacher if I can interview him, once at the end of the first week and then again at the end of the second week. The purpose of the interview is to collect more data and evidence related to what I have observed and to hear his thoughts on my observations and the content that was taught. This will help me to gain insight into the methodology of his work and bring me closer to answering my research question. This data will be recorded either in writing or as a voice recording, with the teacher's consent. All of the above will take place in one classroom. All of the findings will be regarded as potential evidence.*
>
> *I regard an interview as being a prepared conversation with set questions designed to purposely collect evidence concerning a certain topic.*
>
> *A good interview consists of questions that are open-ended, questions that require more than a yes or no answer. A good interview should also rest on trust that has built up between the interviewer and the interviewee.*
>
> *My interview questions will be set up in a particular sequence. These questions will move from practical to more theoretical, from simple to more complex, as the investigation goes on. One thing that I constantly ask myself while devising interview questions is will I learn something from these questions and how is it relevant to my investigation?*
>
> *There are different ways in which to conduct an interview, but I will make use of an interview guide. An interview guide allows me to come up with a very precise list of broad questions that will allow me to explore my research question and probe the interviewee for answers. It has few restrictions and does not confine me to one topic alone.*

When planning interviews in this way, I need to create interview categories that will make it easier to group similar themes and ideas together. I have created these categories in a way that will allow me to gain insight into my research question.

Step 4

The next step is to describe the observation and interview guides and how they will be used. We have considered this in some detail in Chapters 5 and 6.

RESEARCH SITE

Choice of research site is a crucial factor in the investigation. Nonetheless, it can be described briefly at this point in the research report; it will be investigated in great detail later. What should be included in this description is a sketch of the location of the school, the community it serves, the classroom that will host the researcher, the class teacher, and any features of the curriculum and approach to teaching relevant to the focus of the inquiry. Finally, the advantages and limitations of the chosen site for pursuing the research question should be briefly assessed.

RESEARCH ETHICS

The research plan needs to demonstrate an awareness of how sensitively and responsibly classroom research needs to be conducted. What is most useful for this purpose is a set of thoughtfully crafted guidelines that the researcher intends to follow. The following is Kathy's code of conduct:

Being allowed into a classroom to conduct observations is a great privilege. I need therefore to take responsibility for myself and ensure that I cause no harm while in the classroom. When in the classroom I will act in an ethical way through the following steps:

From the first encounter with the teacher I will be upfront and honest about the orientation of my research. Only through my honesty will the teacher be able to give me informed consent to any request.

While in her classroom and outside it I will need to respect the class and the teacher's privacy by not casually repeating to others what happened in the classroom. At no point will I ever attempt to deceive the teacher.

I will not make inappropriate remarks on any social or cultural issues, such as nationality or dress code.

As previously mentioned, it is imperative that I have as little impact as possible on what happens in the classroom. In no way will I try to manipulate the students or the teacher to change the outcome of a situation.

In essence I believe that during all my interactions with the class and the teacher the most important word to keep in mind is 'respect'. As long as I act in a respectful way towards the school, the students and all the teachers, I will be behaving in an ethical way.

PURPOSES AND EXPECTATIONS

This final section of the research plan reflects briefly on the purposes and expectations implicit in conducting and reporting on the investigation. Students have found it useful to distinguish between three kinds of purpose: personal, practical and theoretical. Here is Fay's attempt to clarify her purposes.

The most obvious reason for doing a thesis is as a means to obtain a certain qualification. Nevertheless, there are other purposes. I have divided this section into three parts: personal purposes, practical purposes and research purposes.

Personally, I am writing this thesis as a final-year research assignment to bring me one step closer to obtaining my Bachelor of Education degree, and to research a question of interest to which I have no answer as yet.

Practically, I am writing this thesis to reach a certain academic level. Finishing this research assignment is one of my many goals and will bring me a great sense of achievement. More so, I will be embracing the useful outcome of my research by making use of all the skills that I have learnt in writing, teaching and researching.

My purpose for doing this research with my particular question in mind is to enable me to convert theory into something practical. I also want to gain insight into and unpack the reasons why we use certain methodologies in teaching. I do not want to do things in a certain way simply because it works. I want to know why these methods work and how they work within the classroom.

Both Kathy's account of research ethics and Fay's account of research purposes are personal ones. They reflect some reading on these two subjects but they are personal statements, not repetitions of good practice prescribed in textbooks.

SUMMARY OF KEY POINTS

- Clearly state and justify your research theme, introducing the central ideas around which your investigation is focused and back this up with key quotations.

- Organise your commentary on your preliminary readings.

- Clearly match your choice of research methods to your research question.

- Describe your research site.

- Create your own ethical code of conduct.

- Define your purposes and expectations.

8 Reviewing your research process

In order to understand any human phenomenon we must investigate it as part of the context within which it lies.

Pamela Maykut and Richard Morehouse (1994, p 68)

INTRODUCTION

Assume that the detailed research plan outlined in the last chapter has been implemented in the real world of the classroom. Assume that you have been immersed in this classroom for at least two weeks and that though your observation and interview guides have received harsh reality checks and have required improvisation, you have emerged with rich research data, still to be organised and analysed.

A formal research report requires a frank review of this implementation process. A critical reader needs to know how the research plan survived classroom reality. This review needs to include an account of problems encountered and improvisations required. These matters may have a bearing on the quality of the data generated and on the nature of the conclusions reached.

STRUCTURING THE REVIEW

As with all aspects of the research report, some structure is required for your review. This chapter follows the outline described in the format introduced in Chapter 2 and considers how you might provide a retrospective report on the following six areas of implementation.

1. How you organised access to your research site.
2. How you carried out the interviewing process, how you used your interview guides and how you recorded and processed your data.
3. How you carried out the observation process, how you used your observation guides and how you recorded and processed your data.
4. How you attempted to ensure the accuracy of your data.
5. How the research question might have changed or developed during the data collection process.
6. The strengths and limitations that emerged in your research plan.

Each area is discussed briefly, once again drawing on examples of how Kathy and Fay have dealt with them.

ACCESS TO THE RESEARCH SITE

What is required here is a brief account of the conditions relating to access to the research site that might impinge on the process and outcomes of the investigation. This would include any formal rules governing research in public or private schools, as well as all informal undertakings, and should include a statement of the code of ethics the researcher aims to adhere to. Initial contact with the school and preparatory visits to the school and classroom before beginning the investigation should be described, as well as the attitude of the class teacher to her classroom becoming a research site. Finally, the advantages and limitations of the school and the classroom for your particular investigation should be assessed.

THE INTERVIEWING AND OBSERVATION PROCESSES

We have already examined at some length Kathy and Fay's methods of putting their research questions to work by means of interview and observation guides. What is required in a review of research process are the kinds of frank, factual accounts they gave of using these guides in practice, including the surprises and difficulties encountered that led to changes of tactic.

What stood out in Kathy's data collection process was the enthusiastic role of the class teacher in shaping the theoretical direction of the investigation, the abandonment of both interview and observation guides and her invention of a new formal system to classify examples of predicaments. All these factors would have a bearing on the outcomes of her research and therefore needed to be reported on.

In Fay's case, what was significant was her very tight control of the research agenda, the helpful but restricted role of the class teacher, the abandonment of her observation guide in favour of a flowing day by day narrative account of lesson development, and her decision to record research data in both 'raw' and 'cooked' forms. Again, all these factors would influence research outcomes and therefore warrant recording.

In particular, you should highlight any factors that, in your view, might have restricted or biased your collection and interpretation of data.

ENSURING THE ACCURACY OF RESEARCH DATA

In this section you should report on the steps you took to check the validity of your data, particularly by means of cross-checking and testing the accuracy of your record of observation and interviews. One approach is to recruit the class teacher as a first reader of observation and interview reports. This was Fay's decision:

> *I grappled with the issue of accuracy and eventually came to a conclusion. Clearly and neatly, I wrote out my day-to-day observational notes and gave them to my teacher to read through and correct what he felt needed to be corrected. At the end of my first interview, my teacher told me that he would like to assist me in my research where possible. I took this as an opportunity to ask him if he would like to read through my findings. He agreed, and I presented him with the draft of my findings closer to the end of the second week, when most of my data had been collected. A few minor changes were made here and there and I feel comfortable enough to say that my data is accurate.*

However, there are further methods that could be reported here: the method of recording both interviews and observations, whether by using sound recorders or note taking or both; and the checking of transcriptions and quotations against original sound recordings. In addition, the principles guiding the selection and organisation of research data need to be made clear. A critical reader needs to understand how the brief summary of data they are presented with was arrived at. This will be considered in detail in the following chapter.

PRESSURE ON THE RESEARCH QUESTION

Fay reported on the stability of her research question as follows:

> *No changes were made to my research question, even though I doubted whether I had collected enough data to be able to answer my question. This was, throughout my research weeks, my biggest concern. I am holding onto my research question and will try to answer it as best as I possibly can. Will there be a change in the near future? I have not a clue. But for now, my question remains in its original form.*

However, this is by no means always the case and any changes to the research question, however small and innocent, need to be recorded and explained. Almost every researcher has at some point faced the experience of seeing his or her question as impossible to answer, faced with the limitations of the data that are becoming evident.

STRENGTHS AND LIMITATIONS OF THE RESEARCH PLAN

This final section requires a very general assessment of how an elaborate research plan devised before entry to the research site has survived in practice. The actual research context requires pragmatic responses to what is happening rather than a theoretical detachment. Kathy put it like this:

> *I felt that my research plan gave me solid ground to stand on. I entered the classroom with a clear understanding of what I was seeking. However, while the plan helped to clarify my understanding of a research approach, research methods and interviewing, in practice I focused less on the theory and rather worked in a way that I felt comfortable.*

It was the need to work in '*ways that felt comfortable*' that drove what was the major revision of research plans for both Kathy and Fay. This was their abandonment of their carefully prepared observation guides in favour of a more intuitive response to what was happening in the classroom. It is experiences such as these that need frank recording in the review of the research process.

GENERAL GUIDELINES

The review of the implementation of the research plan is a kind of stock-taking. It need not be long but it does need to be a frank, warts-and-all account. The unexpected is much more interesting and probably more important than the expected. Difficulties encountered and failures to achieve expectations need honest recording.

Its most important purpose is to provide a critical reader with a sense of the strengths and limitations of the inquiry that may have a bearing on the quality of the data collected and its eventual interpretation and analysis.

SUMMARY OF KEY POINTS

- Be honest about the problems you encountered, the improvisations required and the validity of the data generated.

- Structure your review logically and carefully to reflect the key areas suggested in this chapter.

Organising your research data

*Organising is what you do before you do something, so
that when you do it, it is not all mixed up.*

A A Milne (1926)

INTRODUCTION

Two weeks in the research classroom produces a mass of observation and interview data. It is necessary to find some way to order this mass of information, not only for the purposes of the final research report but, more importantly, as a step towards a concluding analysis of the data. But how is this to be done? In this chapter I attempt to answer this question by:

- considering the principles underlying the organisation of data;
- examining Kathy and Fay's strategies for organising their data;
- discussing both approaches;
- drawing out some general guidelines.

SOME KEY PRINCIPLES

Raw versus cooked

The rationale for producing a data summary is the assumption that the collection of data precedes the analysis of data: one collects information before one makes sense of it. The problem with this assumption is that there is no such thing as 'raw data', data that is innocent of interpretation. We can neither collect nor summarise data without some prior interpretation of the data. Collection presupposes selection, and summarising presupposes ordering in accordance with some selective principle.

A useful fiction

Though the idea of collecting raw data and deferring interpretation to a later stage is a fiction, it may turn out to be a useful fiction. There is a case for seeing the summary of research data as 'initial' or 'tentative': as a step towards the fuller analysis that is the task of the concluding section of the research report. It should enable and not pre-empt the more probing and systematic analysis that lies ahead. The task of the data summary is to structure a mass of rough and untidy data, without trying to pretend that we are not involved in interpretation. This requires the invention of a *framework* of some kind.

Possible frameworks

Frameworks differ in the degree to which they favour keeping data as 'raw' as possible or engaging in a 'cooking' process. Some data summaries can be described as 'raw' while others are 'cooked', while others fall in between. Those that are 'cooked' have in fact embarked on the task of final analysis.

Chronology

The researcher who favours a 'raw' form of organisation tends to fall back on simple chronology. He or she will give a day by day summary of classroom observation data, and a question by question account of interview data. Analysis will be deferred. The advantage of this approach is its immediacy. The data remains fresh and flowing, in a form that does not pre-empt future analysis. But it does not assist it either.

Invention of categories

The researcher who wants to make intellectual sense of the data through his or her summary structure will find chronology inadequate. The researcher will tend to make use of his or her observation and interview categories (or invent new categories) to order the data. The advantage of this approach is that an important step has been taken towards data analysis. The potential disadvantage is that categories that have emerged at too early a stage in the research process may prevent fresh ways of interpreting the data from emerging.

EXAMINING KATHY'S SUMMARY OF OBSERVATION DATA

Kathy introduced the summary of her observation data as follows.

Every day during my period of observation I observed the teacher presenting a lesson. In the case of my host teacher the lesson involved a large number of questions; these questions involved the children in the lesson. This dynamic of interactive learning over the duration of the lesson I have chosen to define as the teacher's 'story' of the classroom. While there is class involvement 'the story' is always led by the teacher, therefore making it predominantly the teacher's story. In each story the teacher placed predicaments for the children. These predicaments were always present as without them the children would not be challenged and there would be no learning.

The following summary of observations shows the different forms and uses of these predicaments and the pitfalls that they can create.

In an attempt to lay out the data I have selected in a coherent way I have chosen to group similar predicaments together under broad headings.

What she has done, in terms of her organising framework, is go far beyond her original observation and interview categories. She has, in fact, invented an original system for classifying classroom 'predicaments':

1. *Predicaments which permeate the lesson.*

2. *Predicaments that cause problems.*

3. *Predicaments with purpose.*

4. *Predicaments which perplex.*

5. *Predicaments of perception.*

In her data summary, she defines, explains and gives vivid examples of each form of predicament, drawing selectively on her observation and interview data to do so. This is far more than a data summary: she has embarked on a systematic analysis of her data and an answer to her research question. She describes what she has done as a *'tentative exploration of her categories'*, which will be further analysed in her concluding chapter.

KATHY'S INTERVIEW DATA

Kathy's summary of interview data is similarly analytical. She focuses on the teacher's theoretical contributions to her understanding of 'predicaments' and how they function in pedagogic terms. She is particularly concerned with how those contributions by the teacher deepen her own initial grasp of predicaments. In particular, she recognises the importance of the following statements by the teacher:

'The age of the child will have a huge impact on his or her engagement with any predicament presented to them.'

'It is important for the teacher to "take the predicament out of thinking and into feeling" allowing the child to "take ownership of their work."'

Teacher contributions such as these deepen her understanding of predicaments and refine her developing classification system. This is why she selects them for her summary. Refining the system devised to organise her data has become her major research task.

DISCUSSION OF KATHY'S APPROACH

Summary versus analysis

In both sections of her data summary Kathy is busy writing her final chapter. The question that arises is the following: what will Kathy do when she finally and formally embarks on the analysis of her data? Has she not already done this, in the form of an extremely well-cooked data summary? Or is there more to come – a further stage of interpretation and analysis?

Narrative accounts

Note that Kathy has not excluded narrative accounts from her summary. These occur *within* the categories of her classification system. They take the form of brief passages showing how a particular form of predicament works in practice. Such passages give clear and lively examples of classroom practice.

However, her classification system prevents us (and may be preventing her) from seeing how predicaments work over a period of time in the wider context of ongoing teaching and learning. She may, however, be able to use her model for this purpose in her final, analytical chapter.

EXAMINING FAY'S SUMMARY OF OBSERVATION DATA

The following is an abbreviated version of Fay's introduction to her report on her observation data:

Throughout my stay in Class 4 at the school, the teacher was in the process of teaching the geography main lesson. I arrived on the first day of this new main lesson. The teacher had different focus points throughout the main lesson, namely weather and direction.

During my research, I recorded only what I felt was relevant to my question and useful towards my understanding of my theme. I tried to keep interpretations limited in this section. What I considered to be significant interpretations, I have put in brackets. Chapter 3 will be devoted to further interpretation and analysis.

> *I decided the best way in which to record my observation data was to do a day by day write up. For my research purposes, I clearly specified what subjects or sections of the main lesson I observed. At the end of each day I created a table in which I summed up the day's observations under my five observation categories. This allowed me to select only what is needed for my chapter three and to give the reader a better understanding of what I was trying to observe.*

Fay's data summary is more complicated, detailed and meticulous than Kathy's. It includes 'raw' and 'cooked' sections; and it consciously demonstrates the process of moving between chronological and analytical accounts.

The key features of her method of summarising are as follows:

- It takes lesson content seriously. An intellectual grasp of how children engage with a particular subject is seen as important.
- It is selective rather than inclusive; as she notes: *'I recorded only what I felt was relevant to my question and useful towards my understanding of my theme'.*
- It attempts to *'keep interpretations limited'* and, in addition, to signal the distinction between data and interpretation. Fay makes a deliberate effort to defer analysis to a later chapter.
- It moves from 'raw' to 'cooked' presentations of data in an interesting way. For each of her ten days of observation, she first produces what she calls *'a day by day write up'* in chronological form. She follows this with *'a table in which I summed up the day's observations under my five observation categories'*. She has two clearly stated purposes in doing this:
  - to highlight what she thinks she will need for her final, analytical chapter; and
  - *'to give the reader a better understanding of what I was trying to observe'.*

What follows is an abbreviated version of one of Fay's ten daily data summaries (Day 7) in its two stages: narrative and tabular.

Day 7: Narrative account

MAIN LESSON

Observation walk: The teacher guided the children through all their observation walks but today, the teacher told the class that he would like to hear the observations from them. He asked the children one by one what they could observe. The teacher asked the children who were speaking to be specific and clear. After the observations, the teacher started asking the children in which direction certain places were from where they were standing, for example, the school building was East from where they were standing.

Register/recall: When the children returned to the class, the teacher took the register. Along with calling the child's name, the teacher would ask the child a question related to direction by asking him or her where certain objects were within the classroom and where certain children sat within the classroom. The child had to answer using the four directions. He also asked certain children to establish where the E, W, N and S sides were within the classroom. These children were given a cardinal point to put up on the wall.

At one point, the teacher asked the children if they could guess where the SE corner of the classroom was. The children used logic and pointed out the wall between the South side and the East side

They were given their geography main lesson books to complete their weather report for Day 7. The children always measured the shadow pole in centimetres with a measuring tape. The teacher took the same amount of steps heel to toe inside, as he took to measure the shadow pole outside. As the teacher took a step, the children measured with the measuring tape.

Once the children completed their weather reports, they started to draw a compass. The teacher drew the skeleton of the compass on the board prior to the lesson. He told the children to first draw a big circle in the middle of their page, filling the page. Then the children needed to draw a cross within the centre of the circle. While the children were drawing the compass skeleton from the board, the teacher walked up to the board and went over all the lines with chalk. This gave the children a clear idea of how to draw this compass skeleton. The teacher used different colours for the different direction points on the compass.

Every so often, when the teacher wanted to add something new to the drawing, he would ask: 'Hands up! Who is still busy?' Judging by the children's response to this, he would either move on or wait a while longer for everyone to catch up.

Day 7: table format

Table 9.1 Day 7 account in table form (only one content area is included)

Content	Prior skills (known)	New skills (unknown)	Methodology	Activity
Main lesson	• The children have observation skills. • Children can: - record what they have observed; - write a weather report; - be specific about the position of things; - ascertain direction within an open space.	• Children will be able to identify the four cardinal points on a compass as well as the in between directions. • They will also be able to establish which direction comes where on a compass, as well as the weather conditions that you will find when travelling in these directions. • The children will be able to identify the conditions of the winds coming from the in between directions.	• The teacher followed the living experience method and still took the children on their observation walk. • What the children observe remained the same, but the way in which they spoke of and recorded their observations became more geographic. • The teacher referred back to the story and the four children whenever weather conditions of the four main directions were brought up. • He made good use of recall and repetition to bring the work across to the children.	• 1st activity: the children completed a weather report. • 2nd activity: the children drew a compass into their main lesson books with the four cardinal points and the in between directions.

FAY'S INTERVIEW DATA

Fay's approach to summarising her interview data is completely different from Kathy's. She is not at all selective. She simply records, chronologically, everything the teacher says in response to each of her prepared questions. In her first interview, all her questions relate logically to her research question and make use of her pre-planned observation and interview categories. They are intellectually demanding but the teacher provides clear and penetrating answers. However, he adds nothing of his own; he appears to raise no questions.

The second interview is quite different. It is based on classroom observations. Observed events of the previous week are probed for clarification and deepened understanding. These two approaches complement each other. The first of the examples that follow is from the first interview. The second is from the second interview.

Example 1: derived from the research question

Question: When this specific content of this geography main lesson is over, what are the new skills and abilities that the children will have learnt?

Answer: 'Hopefully the aims of the main lesson, which would be special orientation in their own space and environment. They should be able to know the directions, they should be able to draw simple maps from a bird's-eye view and have more of a feeling of their spatial surroundings. So if they go for a swim at the pool, they will be able to pick up there is a playground there, there is a gate there, the water is over here. So that they've got that kind of picture. I want to in this main lesson also do the winds so that the children get an idea of the direction they are coming from, the clouds and the different types of clouds that you get. They can maybe wake up in the mornings and determine what the weather is going to be like judging by the clouds and the direction it is coming from and going to. If you look at studying the plant kingdom, they will not have an idea of it this year, but when it comes to the observational side of that main lesson, they will have developed some skills of observing phenomena and comparing things.'

Example 2: derived from classroom observation

Question: How do you deal with the children's different levels of understanding of the work? Particularly when it comes to direction, some children are still not clear as to where the different directions are?

Answer: 'I do not necessarily worry about it too much if the children do not understand the work straight away. My feeling is that they all catch up at the end of the day. Like with this, for example, I have got no doubt that by the end of the year, those that do not know, will have picked it up when we continue with the next one or two geography main lessons that we will be doing concerning direction. We are doing mirror imaging where I face them and point to the left and they have got to point to the right, same thing, direction but tricky. But they are all going to get it at some point or the other.'

DISCUSSION OF FAY'S APPROACH

Two distinct parts

Fay's summary of observation data consists of two distinct parts:

1. a detailed chronological narrative that takes the form of a fresh, accessible, daily account of classroom conversation and interaction;
2. a 'translation' of this narrative into an abstract form based on a model derived from her research question.

A dynamic model

This approach enables her to interweave raw and cooked data and to show how the first is transformed into the second. Her abstract model is able to do this because it is not simply a list of headings under which to collect similar kinds of data. It is a dynamic model, interpreting chronological events over a ten-day period in a logical sequence. This enables her to take the flow of engagement with lesson content seriously.

Her research question requires her to grasp the sequence of operations involved when children move from prior to new knowledge. It is her tentative model of this sequence that dictates the logical framework employed in each of her tables. This logical ordering of data, day by day, will provide her, she hopes, with the evidence she requires to explain an intellectual transition that she finds intriguing.

SUMMARISING THE DATA: GENERAL GUIDELINES

Once again, there are no set rules. However, some data summaries work better than others and some guidelines do emerge from the two cases we have examined.

Two purposes of the data summary

It is important to clarify the two purposes of a data summary. The first is the formal expectation that, in a research report, some presentation of data should precede analysis and conclusions. The second – and the far more substantial purpose – is that the summary must move the analysis forward: it must facilitate the analysis of the data that is the next step in the research process.

Over-cooking and under-cooking

In achieving this purpose, the method devised to order the data is crucial. Under-cooking defers analysis to the final section of the research report without helping it. Over-cooking may have the effect of prematurely freezing the data. The categories used for organising the data may pre-empt further and deeper analysis.

Frozen categories

The most harmful procedure is to invent observation and interview categories at the start of the research process, employ the same categories to organise the data summary, and then use these categories once again to structure the final analysis. This is not a recipe for intellectual flexibility and open-minded exploration. The framework chosen for the data summary should not be allowed to claim the status of a final classification. It has to remain tentative and subject to questioning and revision.

Narrative elements

Furthermore, summaries should not exclude narrative elements. These are essential for capturing and communicating classroom life and for keeping data 'alive' and problematic.

How data is summarised has serious implications for the form that the data analysis will take in the final stage of the research report. Unfortunately, these implications are not likely to be perceived in advance.

SUMMARY OF KEY POINTS

- Your data summary and the method you devise for ordering your data should facilitate the analysis of data and promote deeper critical thinking about it.

- Your framework for the data summary should remain flexible.

- Include narrative elements in the summary to bring your data to life.

10 Analysing your research data

A conclusion is the final phase of an argument, the moment when all the pieces coalesce, and something new has been created.

Michael Newman (2014, p 4)

INTRODUCTION

The analysis of research data is the final stage of the research report. This task requires you to reflect in a systematic way on what you have found significant in your research data in order to shape an answer (or answers) to your research question. You need to get to the heart of what your data really means, draw ideas together and work towards some kind of conclusion. In intellectual terms, it is the most challenging and potentially satisfying chapter. It is also the part of the research report that researchers, particularly novice researchers, find most difficult to write. This chapter moves through the following stages:

- why do researchers find the *analysis and conclusion* stage difficult?;
- a possible strategy for avoiding these difficulties;
- an examination of how Kathy and Fay actually tackled this task;
- what we can learn from them;
- some general guidelines for analysing data.

WHY IS THE FINAL CHAPTER A CHALLENGE TO WRITE?

The task of analysis and conclusion comes at the end of a long process of reporting on the collecting, interpreting, weighing and organising of research data. I have depicted the stages of the research report in this simple four-stage model.

1. Research design and theoretical framework.
2. Observation and interviews: A review of this process.
3. Selection and ordering of research data.
4. Interpretation and analysis of research data. Conclusion.

The first three stages of the research report require researchers to:

- give a full description and explanation/justification of the research plan;
- provide a critical review of the process of data collection;
- produce a summary of the data acquired.

Cognitive gear shift

The above three tasks are, in the main, forms of narration and summary. But in the final stage the rules change. Here the researcher is required to do something different – engage in conceptual work at the highest level. In the terms of Bloom's Taxonomy (Bloom et al, 1956), this would involve *analysis, synthesis* and *evaluation*. And this cognitive gear shift is challenging. What novice researchers have not had much experience of is the creating of theoretical frameworks that might help convert *narrative* into *analysis*.

If researchers don't know how to move beyond their data summaries, the simplest thing would be to simply rehash and elaborate upon these summaries. The final chapter becomes, essentially, a repetition of the second. The task of final analysis is effectively ducked and fresh insights that cut across old categories are prevented.

WHAT STRATEGIES ARE AVAILABLE?

Avoiding the rehash of data

How can the tendency to reduce analysis to a rehash of collected data be avoided? The answer lies in the way in which the final chapter is *structured*. The problem with the re-use of old frameworks is twofold:

1. old frameworks tend to push the final chapter into 'collection mode';
2. old frameworks reduce analysis to the task of re-collecting data in a neat and systematic way.

The result is that old frameworks restrict intellectual movement and fresh focus. Most important of all, they restrict argument.

Beginning with the research question

What the process of analysis requires is some form of argument. The researcher needs to design an intellectual task for the final chapter. It is clear that the goal of such a task is to arrive, through a process of reflection, at an adequate answer to the research question. And the obvious starting point is the *research question* itself. To begin with, the research question needs to be restated and a fresh attempt made to ask how best to answer it.

Creating a sequence of developing steps

The task of analysis requires a sequence of developing steps. There are two useful approaches:

1. The first is to create a list of logical steps in a possible argument – a sequence of steps to be worked through in order to reach a considered answer to the research question.
2. The second is to conceive of this task as a series of sub-questions that would need to be answered as a route towards answering the research question.

In either case, sequential argument would displace data classification. We shall return to a detailed consideration of *how* this might be done after examining how Kathy and Fay tackled the task of analysing their data and concluding their research reports.

HOW HAVE KATHY AND FAY TACKLED THE ANALYTICAL TASK?

Because of the marked differences in how they have organised their research data, Kathy and Fay begin their final chapters at different starting points.

Kathy has already completed a sophisticated analysis of her data, using a classification system of her own invention. The question is whether she can move beyond this to a further stage in the analytical process.

Fay has arrived at the end of the data summary process with two forms of interpretation: a compressed narrative account of ten days of teaching and learning; and an abstract model of this account. She has left herself more room for manoeuvre.

EXAMINING KATHY'S APPROACH

Step 1: Kathy's introduction – explaining her new analytical categories

*   Kathy begins with a restatement of her research question: *'How are narrative predicaments created by the teacher and how do the children engage with them?'*
*   She then states that she has devised a simpler and more comprehensive way of looking at her classification of narrative predicaments than that used in her data summary.
*   She explains the logic of her new analytical framework:

These three categories essentially look at predicament as the building blocks of the story. Predicament is essential in every story and the three predicament types I have identified each play a different role in the classroom story.

- Finally, she states the task of her closing chapter:

> *In chapter 3 I will summarise these new categories as well as look at predicament and the advantages it holds in the classroom.*

Step 2: putting her new analytical categories to work

Kathy's second step is to use her new categories in order to produce a final analysis of her data. She first presents her new system in compressed, tabular form:

> *To create a summarised, visual representation of the three predicament types I have created a basic table to help clarify the difference between the three:*

Predicament type	Level of frequency	One-word description	Impact on story
Routine	1	Foundation	Allows story to flow
Maintenance	2	Learning	Momentum of story
Intervention	3	Problem	Derail story

1 = most frequent, 3 = least frequent

> *This table represents three different types of predicaments and ranks them according to the frequency of occurrence in the classroom story and what effect they have on the story of the classroom.*

She then defines each of the three types of predicament, explaining their purposes or unintended consequences in the classroom.

- ***Routine predicaments*** *are present throughout the school day. The teacher creates these kinds of predicaments to keep the class under control so that learning may occur. If these predicaments were not present in the classroom the children would have difficulty identifying the boundaries of the classroom, what behaviour is acceptable and what is not.*

- ***Maintenance predicaments*** *are created by the teacher to facilitate learning. They often take the form of questions where the teacher draws knowledge* *out and imparts knowledge through a discussion with the class or in a task such as completing a worksheet or doing work in the main lesson book. These tasks and questions are predicaments that are specifically formulated by the teacher to help the children learn.*

- ***Intervention predicaments*** *are predicaments where the teacher has created and presented the predicament to the class but the class's reaction shows that something was incorrect with the predicament. Intervention predicaments occur when the teacher has created a predicament that is not suitable for the class.*

Finally, drawing on her data, she proceeds to give concrete examples of each predicament and explain in some detail how each 'works' in the classroom context.

Step 3: reflecting on her new grasp of predicaments

The third step in Kathy's process is to reflect on her new understanding of predicaments. She does this in three stages:

1. Firstly, she analyses the inevitable fluidity and shifts in the nature of predicaments, given the complexity of classroom dynamics.
2. Secondly, she considers, again with the use of examples, the importance of the teacher correctly recognising predicament shifts and acting accordingly.
3. Finally, she stresses the need for the teacher to recognise the pedagogic functions of predicaments and ensure that they are 'working' as effectively as they might.

Step 4: asking the key questions

Kathy's final step is to raise a series of key questions, all of them pedagogic. She uses this method to engage in a final analysis of her data.

- *Why are predicaments crucial for learning?*

- *Are all predicaments good?*

- *What makes a predicament good and what would make it bad?*

- *Was the predicament created useful or not?*

Her considered answers to these questions provide the culmination of her investigation. In effect, she closes by writing a reflective essay on the pedagogy of predicaments. In so doing, she synthesises all her previous thinking and gets to the heart of her research question.

Her final move is to acknowledge very briefly the limitation of her teacher-centred approach, and to recognise the road not followed in her investigation. She has not looked at the predicaments the children create for the teacher and for one another.

DISCUSSION OF KATHY'S APPROACH

Creating a more practical framework

Against the odds, given her well-cooked data summary, Kathy has succeeded in creating a new framework for analysis. She has recognised the limitations of her earlier one, especially in grasping the dynamics of classroom interaction. She believes her new, simpler framework has more practical use.

Steps in an argument

Kathy has designed a logical sequence of steps for her final chapter and she moves through these one by one. In this way the chapter becomes a considered argument leading towards a conclusion.

Series of key questions

She has posed a series of key questions to explore the practical applications of her theoretical work, constructing a pedagogical case for the importance of predicaments.

Critical reflection

She has reflected on her analysis and recognised its limitations. And she has answered, in a unique and unpredictable way, her research question.

EXAMINING FAY'S APPROACH

Step 1: Fay's introduction

Fay begins by restating her research question: *'How is narrative methodology used to connect the known to the unknown in a Waldorf main lesson?'* She then defines her task for her final chapter as follows:

My task for Chapter 3 is to try and answer this question through:

- *deepening the analysis of my data;*

- *interpreting that deepened analysis through conversation;*

- *lastly, arriving at a point where I feel ready to conclude.*

Step 2: analysis of observations over ten days in consolidated form

Her second step is to present a fresh, consolidated data summary in tabular form. This is a highly compressed version of her data in a form that mirrors the relationships her research question requires her to explore.

The new table includes five content areas. Within each content area she analyses a four-stage movement:

- from 'prior skills' (known);
- to 'new skills' (unknown);
- through 'methodology';
- through 'activity'.

The purpose of this model is to 'find connections across categories'. She is clearly interested in explanation, not classification. What follows is a shortened version of her new table. Only three content areas are included: 'News', 'Homework' and 'Main lesson'.

Fay's consolidated data summary (extract)

Content	Prior skills (known)	New skills (unknown)	Methodology	Activity
News	The children understood the concept of news. They understood that the information that they were about to share had to be newsworthy. The fire on the	The most interesting thing about these news sessions was that it was not only done with the intention of sharing exciting individual	The teacher never forced a child to share news with their peers. He always allowed the sharing of news to be voluntary. At times the teacher would	Voluntary news sharing. Practice of public speaking.

Content	Prior skills (known)	New skills (unknown)	Methodology	Activity
	mountain was mentioned on several occasions. The teacher created time for news since earlier grades.	news, but that the children can become comfortable with public speaking. Again, this is a growing skill that will develop and keep developing as the child grows.	use narrative methodology to draw on the information being shared during these news sessions, to carry the class from the news to the main lesson of the day.	
Homework	The homework was never given on unknown work. The children already understood at least the basis of the content and had the language ability to read what was required of them or understand what was verbally being instructed to them.	Through these small homework tasks, the children learnt how to work independently. They also learnt how to read and follow instructions, verbal or written. The children worked on new content through old knowledge.	The teacher based all his homework tasks on the main lesson. Homework was given twice during my research period and both those times the homework tasks were taken from stories that were told during the main lesson periods.	The homework activities were always discussed the morning after. The information that the children would give formed part of the introduction to the new main lesson of the day.
Main lesson	The children learnt many prior skills from previous main lessons beginning at class one. To list what their prior skills are would be an enormous task. However, not all of those prior	The children learnt many new skills. The list grew every day. In order for this to happen, prior skills had to be put to practice. (This will be elaborated in my interpretation section.)	It seemed the teacher, when explaining the content, liked to give the children a living experience, but would incorporate the narrative methodology in his activities. The children did their	The activities were the recordings of the observations, the children's weather reports and broadcasts. The teacher started out with a simple recording list

Content	Prior skills (known)	New skills (unknown)	Methodology	Activity
	skills were used at once. A few of them were used per lesson, depending on the content that they were about to learn.		observations and the narrative would come into play when those observations were recorded. However, the teacher created one main story on which he built up his content.	and slowly moved towards the narrative writing through the weather broadcasts.

Step 3: 'a conversation with my data'

She calls her third step 'a conversation with my data'. In this section she attempts to get to the heart of what her data are telling her. She begins this process by stating her key insight:

> I discovered that the connection does not lie between the unknown knowledge and the methodology, but rather that the connection for which I searched lies between the prior skills and the new skills; the known knowledge and the unknown knowledge.

The rest of her analysis is a theoretical exploration of the relationship between these two stages of knowledge. To do this she creates the visual metaphor of 'the swinging bridge' that links the known and the unknown, the concrete and the abstract. Her explanation is speculative and ambitious and is illustrated by specific examples from her data. It includes the following propositions:

- that reasoning takes place when a task requires us to swing between the known and the unknown. This is how new meanings are formed;

- that there is already a deep connection between the two sides. This deep connection lies within the abstract region;

- that narrative methodology is not used to create a connection between the two sides, but rather to enhance the connection that is already there and make it visible to the children;

- *that the child draws intuitively on prior skills and selects what he needs to perform the new tasks required of him;*

- *that the connection between the known knowledge and the unknown knowledge comes into play when this selective process happens.*

Step 4: answering the research question

Her final step is to give a neat theoretical answer to her research question:

In answer to my question, I discovered that between the known knowledge (prior skills) and the unknown knowledge (new skills) lies a deep abstract connection. The role of the narrative methodology is to pick up on and enhance that connection, making an already existing connection visible and concrete to the children.

DISCUSSION OF FAY'S APPROACH

Intellectual curiosity

Fay's primary task throughout her investigation has been to satisfy her intellectual curiosity, not to solve any practical problem. She has achieved this goal; and she has relished becoming a theorist.

Concentrating on connections

Fay has discovered a way of compressing her data into a tabular form that mirrors the relationships implicit in her research question. And she has consistently focused on such possible connections, avoiding the simple collecting and classifying of data.

Short sequence of steps

Like Kathy, she begins her analysis with a restatement of her research question, and devises a sequence of steps towards an answer. Her sequence is a far shorter one. Her analysis is largely compressed within one long theoretical discussion of her intellectual 'discovery'.

Unpredictable answer to the research question

Unlike Kathy, she does not concern herself with the practical implications of her 'discovery'. She is convinced that good theory implies good practice. Like Kathy, she ends by answering her research question and doing so in a unique and unpredictable way.

ANALYSING THE RESEARCH DATA: GENERAL GUIDELINES

What can we learn from the design of Kathy's and Fay's final chapters?

Begin with the research question

- The research question is crucially important to the structure of the final chapter. The purpose of this chapter is to answer your research question as fully and as deeply as your data allow you to.
- Both Kathy and Fay began their concluding analysis with a restatement of the research question, demonstrating that this question remains alive and well. Furthermore, their questions remain alive for the duration of the process of analysis, and continue to give energy, focus and direction throughout the chapter.
- Both researchers return to their research questions at the end of their analyses. They see this as an appropriate way of achieving closure. They offer a brief assessment of their attempt to provide an answer.

Define the task for the chapter

- Answering the research question provides the purpose for the chapter; it does not define the task required to achieve this purpose. Kathy saw this task in the following way:
  - to summarise her newly invented categories;
  - to examine how predicaments work;
  - to explore the pedagogic advantages that classroom predicaments offer.
- Fay defined her task as
  - *'deepening the analysis of my data';*
  - *'interpreting that deepened analysis through conversation';*
  - *'arriving at a point where I feel ready to conclude'.*

Define a sequence of steps to complete the task

- Both researchers carefully design a sequence of tasks that need to be completed before the research question can be answered. They create a logical and manageable framework for their closing argument.
- Kathy's is long and detailed; Fay's very short, but both progress systematically, step by step, and both work effectively. They provide the map for the final analytical journey.

Create a final data summary

- In both cases, towards the beginning of their sequence of tasks, the researchers introduce new, highly compressed, ways of looking at their data. This is important for two reasons.
  - Firstly, the new summary presents old data in a structured form that directly informs the analysis.
  - Secondly, this restatement of data insists on the continuing importance of concrete data, in providing both checkpoints and supporting evidence for the developing argument.

Conclude the analysis

- Kathy closes her research report with a brief reflective essay on the pedagogy of predicaments, which gets to the heart of her research question. And her final move is to acknowledge very briefly the necessary limitations of her 'teacher-centred' approach.
- Fay's final step is to give a terse and elegant theoretical answer to her research question. But in addition she reflects on the significance of the now completed research task for her as a person.
- Both approaches communicate a sense of a job well done, the satisfying but not uncritical completion of a long journey.

SUMMARY OF KEY POINTS

- Analysis of your research data requires you to reflect in a systematic way on what you have found that is significant in order to shape an answer to your research question.

- It involves conceptual work at the highest level, creating theoretical frameworks that might help convert *narrative* into *analysis*.

- Begin with the research question and develop a sequence of steps to be worked through in order to reach a considered answer.

- Create a final version of the data summary to support and strengthen your analysis.

- Give a meaningful, reflective and critical conclusion.

11 Evaluating your research report

*The real voyage of discovery consists not in seeking
new landscapes, but in having new eyes.*

Marcel Proust (2006, p 657)

INTRODUCTION

This chapter has three purposes:

1. to consider how knowledge of final assessment criteria can inform the research process;
2. to consider the key role of evaluation *throughout* the research process;
3. to clarify the various ways in which ongoing evaluation takes place.

The first focus will be on the *summative evaluation* of the research report – its final assessment for examination purposes. I want to argue that it is important for students to have a clear understanding of how their research reports will be assessed. In particular, they need to know, at a reasonably early stage in the research process, what criteria will be used to arrive at a judgement.

However, ongoing *formative evaluation* pervades the conduct of research and the crafting of the report. It is a crucial ingredient in the research process. It includes exposure to good practice, the process of supervision, informal peer assessment and ongoing self-evaluation and self-reflection.

We begin with summative evaluation, and consider, too, its bearing on formative evaluation.

SUMMATIVE EVALUATION

Research reports are formally assessed after their final submission. The assessment process can therefore be seen as outside the remit or concern of research students. This would be a misguided view.

The criteria for evaluating complex crafts – tennis, medical diagnosis, teaching or qualitative research – are acquired in the doing and acquired slowly. They cannot be delivered in advance. Nonetheless, the research student is entitled to a clear understanding of how his or her work will eventually be judged. And a formal declaration of what is at stake when performance is judged might focus the mind greatly even if the criteria involved are not, to begin with, fully understood.

Examining an assessment schedule

The following assessment schedule, devised and refined by faculty and external examiners at the Centre for Creative Education, is shared with my students at an early stage in their research journey. I am not advocating the use of this particular schedule: each tertiary institution will have its own version. I use it simply as a practical example of the usefulness of a carefully designed rubric.

Table 11.1 Marking schedule for the research report

Descriptions	Mark allocation
Research topic and question: The student has a personal grasp of the research topic. A suitable question has been clearly defined. The possible outcomes of the investigation are clearly explained.	10
Preliminary reading: Relevant articles are discussed to provide a tentative frame of reference for the investigation.	10
Research design / plan: The research perspective is explained. The procedures chosen for data collection are fully described and clearly justified in relation to the research question. Research ethics are clarified.	10
Research implementation: The process of data collection is fully described and any improvisations in research procedure explained. The chosen research design is evaluated in the light of the experiences during the data collection process.	10
Data presentation: Data is systematically organised and summarised in ways that distinguish them from interpretations and conclusions.	20
Analysis and conclusions: The interpretation of the data is presented in a systematic, reflective and open-minded way. Interpretations and conclusions are supported by the data and related to the literature.	25
Researcher's voice: The authentic voice of the researcher is present throughout the research report.	5

Table 11.1 *(cont.)*

Descriptions	Mark allocation
Presentation and language: The research report has a coherent structure and is a carefully edited and presentable document, using correct spelling and grammar.	5
Referencing: In-text references and concluding reference list meet academic conventions.	5

Major criteria

This schedule follows the research report format recommended to students and discussed in Chapter 2. Nine criteria are briefly defined and each is given a numerical weighting. Almost half the available marks are allocated to two parts of the report: *data presentation* and *analysis and conclusions*. Students are left in no doubt about what is most valued: the quality of the data and the quality of their interpretation and analysis. And pithy criteria are specified too. Research data have to be summarised in ways that *'distinguish them from interpretations and conclusions'*. And analysis and conclusions have to be *'presented in a systematic, reflective and open-minded way, interpretations and conclusions are supported by the data and related to the literature'*.

These are terse and sophisticated criteria directed at examiners and will certainly not be grasped immediately by students beginning their investigations. But the criteria are there formally, in black and white; they will be referred to, discussed and thought about from time to time, and as the research report takes shape they will become better understood. The key thing is that they are available and explicit.

The crafting of the research plan is given reasonable weight too. *Research design* – including an explanation of the research theme, the definition of the research question, a report on preliminary reading, and an account of the research approach and methods – receives a weighting of 30 per cent.

Here again, sophisticated criteria are specified: *'the procedures chosen for data collection are fully described and clearly justified in relation to the research question'*. And in this case too, the sophisticated criterion of *justification of methods* will be one that will probably be fully grasped only in the doing.

Minor criteria

The three minor criteria are particularly interesting – those that are each worth only five per cent of total marks. Students might well say: *'I won't worry about referencing, presentation and language or something vaguely called "the researcher's voice"'*. But this would be unwise: these minor criteria are tricky ones. They are tricky because unlike all the other criteria they attempt to measure characteristics of the research report that are pervasive. These criteria cannot be applied to specific parts of the report, like *data presentation* or *analysis and conclusion*.

They are also tricky because their light weightings are misleading. Ignore *'presentation and language'* and the research report fails to communicate as an accurate, serious and comprehensible document. In practice, poor language and presentation will leave a negative impression in examiners' minds that, if measured, would far exceed five per cent of the total marks. There is no doubt that professional editing and presentation predispose the examiner to inflate the value of the report as a whole.

The same is true of the *'researcher's voice'*. The impact of a strong, clear and authentic writing style is a key factor in reader engagement. It communicates confident intellectual ownership of the investigation. The report is being written by someone who is personally involved in the story they are telling. There is rapport between the writer and the examiner.

Poor referencing has the same negative effect as poor language and presentation. Both tend to create a general impression that will extend well beyond the formal five per cent status of these criteria. Not all students have mastered the technical skills these criteria require. Referencing conventions are easily learnt. Language and presentation skills are a different matter. Here, help may need to be recruited, possibly throughout the writing process.

THE EXTERNAL EXAMINER'S SUMMATIVE ASSESSMENT

The external examiner has used this marking schedule to submit her summative assessment of Fay's research report. It is reproduced in Table 11.2. Please examine it carefully.

Table 11.2 External examiner's report

External examiner's report	%
Research topic and question 10%	
Your introduction is good, and you arrive at a good, clear research question with a strong motivation. You acknowledge the challenges of researching a complex, abstract question such as this.	70
Preliminary reading 10%	
You engage with the readings very well, and allow them to stimulate your own questions, and to make personal meaning of their ideas. The section is well structured around a series of questions.	70

Table 11.2 (*cont.*)

External examiner's report	%
Research design / plan 10%	
You show a good grasp of the qualitative/quantitative distinction, and engage well with the research literature. Research methods are selected appropriately. There is good, systematic development of questions for the observation and interview schedules. You could have said something about the ordering of observations and interviews. It is also not clear how easily some of the aspects will be observed (the problems with this emerge later). The discussions on validity and ethics are good.	65
Research implementation 10%	
This is very thoroughly described, as well as how adjustments to the methods had to be made along the way. Good, critical self-reflection on the limitations of the observation categories.	70
Data presentation 20%	
Again, this section demonstrates a very good, systematic approach to the research, both 'doing justice' to the richness of the data, as well as thinking ahead to what might facilitate the analysis. It is rather too lengthy and detailed though: it might have been better to have summarised some of the day's observations, and then selected a few key ones to present in detail. I also felt that the story (4 Cardinal Points) should have been presented earlier, as there were a number of references to it that didn't make sense until the reader arrived at the story.	75
Analysis and conclusions 25%	
You make very good use of the table to summarise your findings and prepare for your analysis. You put forward a very interesting, creative argument to explain your findings, through the 'Swinging Bridge' model. This demonstrates a depth of thinking and is to be commended. However, although you do make an effort to link these to your findings, the model and the argument operate at quite a general, abstract level, and their connection with the data is tenuous. The argument is complex and quite difficult to follow.	70
Researcher's voice 5%	
Strong and clear.	70
Presentation and language 5%	
The writing is well done, and very engaging. At times it is a little long and repetitious, and there are a few typo/spelling errors.	65
Referencing 5%	
Need to pay attention to referencing conventions when citing someone in another author's work. Otherwise the referencing is well done, except for three items in the bibliography where the author is referred to as MCJ (unpolished)?	65

External examiner's report	%
General comments:	
Overall, a very dedicated, systematic and creative research report which is strong methodologically, but where the final jump to quite an abstract conclusion was maybe a bit too ambitious.	
Final course work mark 100%	70

Discussion of the summative assessment of Fay's research report

What is striking about this final assessment is the time and care that has gone into it. The examiner's engagement with Fay's report has been a thoughtful and thorough one. Interestingly, she has written her report directly to Fay, rather than to the College that has commissioned it. While the College will use this report, along with one by an internal examiner, in order to assign a grade, Fay will receive a personal copy.

In a formal sense, despite the quality of this report, there is nothing Fay can do with it except note it. It has arrived too late for improvements to the text. But interesting questions arise:

- To what extent has Fay been able to anticipate the examiner's judgements – the examiner's sense of the strengths and limitations of her report? How good has she become at evaluating her own work?
- To what extent might this positive assessment be the result of Fay's mastery of the criteria the examiner values?

It is impossible to give firm answers to these questions but I suggest that Fay, at the end of her research journey, probably has a very good idea of the worth of her report. I think she will be gratified but not surprised by the examiner's judgements. And I think she will also find them entirely comprehensible. This is because the examiner is using criteria familiar to her – criteria that have been considered and applied throughout the research process. Through such use they have slowly become internalised – part of her intuitive way of thinking about her work. She has herself become an evaluator.

Another interesting question is this: will Fay be able to make any future use of this assessment? Again, answers can only be speculative, but I suggest she may well be able to make use of it in the following personal ways:

- through the confidence this assessment will give her in her ability as a researcher, a thinker and a writer;
- in her desire to continue her passion for studying what is happening in her own classroom when she begins teaching;
- possibly in future career choices.

There is, however, one indisputable factual outcome of this assessment. Fay decided to publish her report, in shortened form, in an international journal.

Familiarity with the assessment rubric used by the examiner is therefore crucial. This important prior knowledge makes the criteria used to judge final reports completely predictable, and the actual judgements understandable.

FORMATIVE EVALUATION

I have argued that formative evaluation pervades the crafting of the research report and is a crucial ingredient in the research process. It is both a conscious and an unconscious process, but it is important that it becomes increasingly conscious. In addition to the growing awareness of the summative assessment criteria just discussed, it includes:

- exposure to good practice;
- the process of supervision;
- informal peer assessment and feedback;
- developing a capacity for self-reflection.

Exposure to good practice

This guide is full of examples of good practice, from precisely defined research questions to carefully structured conclusions. The point is to learn to recognise what makes such exemplars good, and this requires their analysis and discussion over time throughout the writing of one's own research report.

However, such brief examples as I have used in this guide cannot replace the sense and feel of an excellent completed research report. And I recommend working through actual printed and bound copies of successful reports at an early stage in the research process.

Supervision as formative evaluation

In Chapter 4 we considered what defining the research question entailed and drew on examples of students' emerging questions to do so. In practice, this process of definition took several days. It was supported in two ways: through interactive class teaching where the criteria for judging a good question were studied; and through individual feedback on early attempts by a research supervisor.

Such individual feedback on developing work is probably the most important part of formative evaluation, for the following reasons.

- Critique is provided at the point at which it is needed, either by personal discussion of the developing text or, most commonly today, by interactive email. One-to-one supervision by email creates an effective virtual classroom.

- Feedback is tailored to solving real problems.
- Criteria are clarified and understood through engagement with such real problems.

Over time, the supervisory process becomes a conversation about learning, one that is consistently evaluative. And through this, the student's capacity for self-evaluation is developed.

Informal peer evaluation: classroom culture

If, in addition to having one-to-one communication with a supervisor, you are fortunate enough to meet regularly with other researchers in a group or classroom setting, a further form of evaluative discourse arises. The 'rules' of communication that govern communication with one supervisor are very different from those that apply to a conventional face-to-face discussion group or classroom. I have made a rough first attempt to compare these *communication modes* in Table 11.3.

Table 11.3 Contrasting modes of communication

	Face-to-face classroom	**Virtual classroom**
Space and time	Constrained by space and time boundaries	Unconstrained by space and time boundaries. The course intrudes into personal time and social space
Dominant mode of communication	Spoken	Exclusively written
Form of social interaction	Public, collective	Private, individual
Focus of assessment	On general participation and performance	On written text only
Judgements	Public, visible to class	Individual, private
Pace of work	General pace of the class	Differentiated, varies from individual to individual
Control	Loose	Tight
Pressure to improve	Low and diffuse	Intense and focused
Judgement of peers	Powerful	Absent
Classroom culture	Public, shared, intuitively understood	Not visible
Lecturer–student relationships	Publicly visible	Private, less visible

Though both communication modes enable self-evaluation, they operate in very different ways. The *face-to-face classroom* is more effective in shaping a shared, publicly accessible *evaluative culture*. Its mode is a verbal one. The judgements of peers are powerful. Confident students will operate more comfortably within it. By contrast, communication in the *virtual mode* is intensely private, mainly in written form, and tailored to an individual researcher and an individual text. Both modes, in their different ways, are extremely effective in creating and supporting the capacity for self-evaluation and self-reflection.

Inevitably, however, any face-to-face classroom will generate a further pattern of communication: *informal, off the record, student-to-student communication*, whether face-to-face or via social media. I have no idea what 'rules' might apply to this 'unofficial' mode of communication. I would guess that such informal discourse would be to some extent subversive, highly personal, humorous, and provide forms of genuine, practical support that the more formal modes do not provide.

Developing a capacity for self-reflection

In her final report to the College on the work of the group of students we have been following, the external examiner made the following comment:

> *Almost all also made very thoughtful critical reflections on their research journeys, and on themselves as researchers; this development of a capacity for 'meta-reflection' is particularly valuable to them as researchers.*

I think this reflective capacity is at least partly the result of requiring these students to write in 'real time'. What they wrote was never 'final' but as good as they could make it at the time. The next stage in their writing would attempt to take stock of the limitations of the present one. So they were always looking back in order to look forward.

Self-reflection is also an important feature of qualitative research: the capacity to examine what one is doing, seeing, thinking and writing. It is a form of intellectual awareness, tolerant and critical simultaneously.

Several of the student researchers whose work we have been looking at ended their research reports with brief passages of self-reflection – on both the research process and on their personal development. Here are two of these reflective passages, written by Fay and Simon:

> *My findings satisfied my curiosity. This research has been vastly different to any other challenge that I have accepted. It was fresh, it was new, it was exciting and definitely thought-provoking but also very intimidating. To me, being able to finish this dissertation is a great achievement at my present academic level. At first, going into the classroom to conduct my research was hard because, after nearly four years of formal training to become a teacher, I had to retrain myself*

and let go of habits that I developed as a student teacher, especially when it came to recording my data. It was only once I learnt to do this that I became a true researcher. As a researcher I was able to see, understand, analyse and interpret things that I would never have been able to as a teacher. These are good spectacles to keep safe in your briefcase, as another way of looking at the world. In my opinion, being a researcher should always be part of being a teacher. As a teacher, you can never know enough and with every new lesson, comes a new research assignment. (Fay)

This research report was a challenge for me. It challenged my writing skills as well as my way of thinking. It challenged me to think more clearly and more theoretically but also to write more clearly and more theoretically. Through these challenges I have gained more confidence as a researcher and as a writer. I feel that through this process I was given the opportunity to improve my personal skills base. I have learnt that I am capable of taking on new and sometimes scary challenges and work with them and in some cases even overcome them in a systematic and organised way. I feel that I have gained so much from this journey of writing a research report. (Simon)

Fay, as in her research report as a whole, is most interested in intellectual engagement. She stresses *'curiosity'* and *'excitement'*. She values the acquisition of a new way of seeing things: the capacity to *'understand, analyse and interpret things that I would never have been able to as a teacher'*. And she wishes to continue to use these new *'spectacles'* in her professional life. Simon is particularly aware of the many skills he has gained; it is the discipline of research that has helped him most. In both cases, looking back in a self-reflective way seems to come easily.

SUMMARY OF KEY POINTS

- Become fully familiar with the final assessment criteria for your research project.

- Embrace the role and benefits of formative assessment throughout the research process.

Proposed format for a research report

PROPOSED STRUCTURE OF RESEARCH REPORT

Chapter 1: research planning and design

(Write Chapter 1 mainly in the past tense)

1. **The research theme:** Give a brief introduction to your research theme and explain why you think it worth investigating.
2. **Preliminary reading:** Give an outline of what you have learnt about your research theme through preparatory reading. Explain which ideas you have found most interesting and useful in helping you to define your research question.
3. **The research question:** Define your research question clearly and explain how you arrived at it.
4. **Purposes and expectations:** Clarify the theoretical purposes of your research (what it is you wish to understand), its practical purposes (ways in which your findings might prove useful) and its personal purposes (possible benefits to you individually).
5. **Research site(s):** Describe your proposed research site(s) and subjects. Given your particular research question, what do you see as the advantages as well as the possible limitations of your research site?
6. **Research design:** Describe and justify the qualitative research approach chosen for your investigation; and explain and justify the particular research methods you have chosen to use.
7. **Research ethics:** Identify the ethical issues you see arising in your particular investigation and explain how you intend to deal with them.

Chapter 2: research process and summary of research data

Part 1: review of the research and data collection process

(In the past tense, probably with brief shifts into present tense where this feels necessary)

Report briefly on how the research was carried out in practice.

Give a clear account of how you implemented your research plan, including problems encountered and improvisations required. The following sub-headings might be useful:

- how you organised access to your research site;

- how you carried out the interviewing process, how you used your interview guides and how you recorded and processed your data;

- how you carried out the observation process, how you used your observation guides and how you recorded and processed your data;

- how you attempted to ensure the accuracy of your data;

- how the research question might have changed or developed during the data collection process;

- ethical issues and how you dealt with these;

- the strengths and limitations that emerged in your research plan.

Part 2: summary of research data

(In the past tense, probably with brief shifts into the present tense where this feels necessary)

Present a well-organised summary (including brief quotations where appropriate) of your research data. You will need to consider the most useful way to structure this summary. Your research question and your interview and observation guides will help you to do this.

Chapter 3: analysis and conclusion

(In the present tense)

Analysis and discussion: Interpret your data in a systematic, reflective and open-minded way, supporting conclusions with reference to the data. You may wish to draw on additional theoretical reading to assist you with this. Indicate what questions require further investigation, identify possible applications of research findings and reflect briefly on your intellectual journey.

Why research in 'real time' matters

INTRODUCTION

This brief paper (which began as an internal discussion document) is an attempt to explore the implications – pedagogical and practical – of applying a 'real time' principle to teaching students how to conduct empirical research and produce a dissertation as part of their undergraduate teacher education programme at the Centre for Creative Education in Cape Town (CCE). A very brief account of the CCE student research programme is necessary to provide the context for this discussion.

THE RESEARCH PROGRAMME AT THE CENTRE FOR CREATIVE EDUCATION

The main task of the Centre for Creative Education is to qualify teachers to teach in Waldorf and mainstream schools through a Bachelor of Education degree course. As part of this course, students are required to submit a formal dissertation on some aspect of primary school education. Over recent years CCE has developed an integrated research programme that has both raised the quality of research and enabled students to meet tight deadlines for the submission of research reports. The features of this programme are as follows:

- The first quarter of the final year is devoted entirely to research. Final research reports are to be submitted before the start of the second quarter.
- All students are required to explore a common research theme. This theme changes every year.
- Within this theme, students pursue individual research questions.
- Theory and practice are completely integrated: instruction in research methods both guides and accompanies the research process.
- Supervision takes the form of detailed formative assessment of students' work, which is submitted, critiqued and revised through rapid email communication.
- Research reports are submitted chapter by chapter, with tight deadlines. Each chapter builds on the previous one and acknowledges and addresses the possible limitations of the previous one. Cosmetic rewriting is discouraged; explicit critical reflection and change of mind are encouraged.

- Research is 'qualitative' not 'quantitative'. It relies on interpretation of evidence and not on measurement and is appropriate for small-scale exploratory investigations in the real-life situation of the classroom.
- The programme takes students through three stages of work:
  - design (including definition of the research question, a literature review and appropriate methodology);
  - implementation (including immersion in a school or classroom situation for systematic data collection over a two-week period);
  - analysis (interpreting research data in a systematic, reflective and open-minded way).

THE 'REAL TIME' DEBATE

It was the critique of student dissertations by an external examiner that forced me to analyse just what it is that convinces me of the importance of 'real time' in student learning (and possibly in all learning). This principle had so quietly and incrementally crept into our research practice at CCE over the last eight years that it had achieved taken-for-granted status. The value of the examiner's query was that it came as a challenge to the 'obvious'.

The key paragraph in the examiner's report I need to address is the following:

> *Most of the reports pointed to a difficulty that students experienced in defining where – in terms of time – they were standing when writing the report. In many cases, their writing reflected a mixture of three standpoints in time – before, during and after the research. It would be helpful if they could be encouraged to write from a more consistent standpoint of after the research had been completed.*

The examiner's position here is the one she is accustomed to, the one that university staff and students assume to be 'normal' and customary. This is the position I worked from when I began teaching and supervising student research at CCE some eight years ago. At that time the students took an introductory course in research methods, designed a research project that interested them, carried out the research and gathered their data, and then, finally, wrote – with hindsight – their research reports. It was the problems that emerged from this conventional approach that over time led to the 'real time' innovation.

PROBLEMS WITH THE CONVENTIONAL APPROACH

The most obvious problem of this approach was that many students were unable to submit their research reports on time. This caused considerable stress, eroded other aspects of the final-year curriculum, made excessive demands on staff time, caused financial problems, and frequently delayed graduation of even able students, sometimes by years. This problem was a particularly severe one for students with poor formal education.

A further obvious problem was that students were not, in fact, able to apply or transfer what they had learnt in their research course to their actual research practice. The gap – chronologically and conceptually – was too big. They had been exposed to research methods in modular, theoretical form; they did not know what its principles meant in terms of practice. These would have to be rediscovered (with difficulty) within the praxis of their own research project. And this lay in the future.

The third obvious problem was that the range of individual and idiosyncratic research topics that students chose to investigate meant that their topics were framed by common-sense assumptions, were under-theorised and were difficult to supervise.

CURRICULUM STRATEGIES

We discovered that the way forward lay in a common research theme, the concentration of research work within a tight time frame, a rigorous support structure and, most crucial of all, a way of integrating theory and practice. *'Real time' became the key mechanism of integration.* In practical terms these innovations worked in the following ways.

The integration of the introductory research module and school-based research

A two-week research module at the start of the final year flowed directly into school-based research. The task of this module was to enable students to write the first chapter of their research reports and submit this (in draft form) within a week after the module ended. The second chapter was due three weeks later, and the final chapter was due two weeks after this. Further research classes were scheduled to support this process. This procedure enabled the research course to be relevant (in 'real time') to each of the three stages students were going through in their research process – *planning and design, data collection and organisation,* and *analysis and discussion.* This was a form of concentration in time and an integration of what had been separate components was the key innovation.

The 'research team' approach

The class became, in fact, a research team, and experienced an apprenticeship in research methods. This apprenticeship involved engagement with a demanding academic text, defining a research question, devising a research plan, and, through all this, grasping what being a researcher entailed. A firm supporting structure was provided by pre-selected texts, sequential tasks and a simple research report format. As work progressed, students developed individual approaches to the common task, introduced new readings and the first person plural became the first person singular.

Research as a process of writing: communication, critique and revision by email

Students were required to become writers from the first moment of the research module. The pressure to write was relentless. To begin with, what was written was examined, critiqued and improved in class. Then, after two weeks, all writing was submitted and critiqued by email with a 24-hour turnaround time. The research teacher became the research supervisor. Though there were strict deadlines for each draft chapter, students could send small sections for comment whenever they wished to. All supervision was by email. There were no meetings. All conversation was both *in* writing and *about* writing.

The principle of writing each chapter in 'real time' sequence

Research reports were submitted chapter by chapter, and these chapters were regarded as final drafts. Chapter 1 was a genuine research plan, written before immersion in the research site. Chapter 2 reported on the actual implementation of this research plan. And Chapter 3 reflected on the significance of the data reported on in Chapter 2. Each chapter was enabled by, and built on, the previous one. And each acknowledged and addressed the limitations of the previous one. Cosmetic rewriting and 'false coherence' were discouraged; explicit critical reflection and justified change of mind encouraged. So research reports were written from three time perspectives in answer to three questions: what do I intend to do; what I have I discovered; and what does this mean? I do not think students were confused by these different positions (as the examiner suggested). I think they experienced them as three consecutive and logical steps towards task completion.

WHY DOES THE PRINCIPLE OF 'REAL TIME' MATTER?

The 'real time' principle is a pedagogic principle. It matters for motivation, for reflexivity and for task completion. All are interrelated.

Motivation

In motivational terms, 'real time' meant 'real task', not preparation for some future task. Students were engaged as a group and individually with a series of real tasks that were achievable by all within a relatively short time. Every small piece of writing submitted was a stage in the completion of the task. Piece by chronological piece, and day by day, each student could see the text of her actual research report becoming a reality. This sense that 'I am writing my actual research report now' was highly motivating: it generated both a strong sense of ownership of the task and a growing sense of confidence in its completion. *This was not preliminary work*: the final report (barring a careful edit) was taking shape in the present tense.

The 'real time' equals 'real task' principle was crucial, I think, in the degree of personal investment visible in the students' work. The external examiner put it like this:

> *I think the biggest strength of these research projects was the deep personal investment and interest of the students in their research questions; this clearly motivated them and enhanced the quality of the research. This personal investment and motivation furthermore translated into a style of writing that allowed them to express a strong sense of their own 'voice'.*

This sense of the authenticity of the research task and of personal engagement in the research journey seems particularly important at a time when some student research work in education at South African universities has been reported to be 'dummy research', going through the motions of research procedure without ownership of and understanding of the research task.

Reflexivity

The customary way of writing a research report is to revise earlier drafts so that these are consistent with the final draft. A position of hindsight, taken at the end of the entire research process, determines which parts of earlier drafts will be retained, modified or omitted. The aim is to produce a coherent, consistent and smooth account of the research process and findings: a persuasive text. In producing such a final text, error, shift of focus, loss of faith in a research question – indeed, critical reflection on an unfolding intellectual process – may be regarded as interference or irrelevance and omitted or concealed.

The examiner made the following comment about the students' capacity for critical reflection:

> *Almost all also made very thoughtful critical reflections on their research journeys, and on themselves as researchers; this development of a capacity for 'meta-reflection' is particularly valuable to them as researchers.*

In my view, it is the requirement to write in 'real time' that licensed and produced such 'meta-reflection'. Such reflection became the necessary substitute for erasure. Inconsistencies needed to be explained rather than concealed. Coherence lay in explicit justification and explanation: an honest text, aware of (and even enjoying) its uneven process of production.

Task completion

Task completion is the most concrete consequence of writing in 'real time'. With very rare exceptions, students completed and submitted their entire research reports within four months. Before the concentration of research in the first quarter of the final year and before the 'real time' stipulation, students had needed at least a year, and some several years, to complete and submit their reports. A major cause of this was that the daunting retrospective task of final report writing was continually deferred. The report was never quite good enough, never quite finished and never quite coherent enough. And other priorities inevitably intervened.

IN CONCLUSION

In concluding this brief case study, I would like to express my appreciation to the examiner who questioned my 'real time' pedagogic fundamentalism and for choosing to see examiners' reports as opportunities for reflection and dialogue. It has been a long time since I was last required to explore dearly held pedagogic assumptions, and I have enjoyed the process.

Notes

1. *My appreciation to Associate Professor Linda Cooper of the University of Cape Town who, as external examiner, sparked the above discussion.*
2. *A full account of the student research programme at the Centre for Creative Education can be found in the following paper:* Millar, C, Melmed, T, Nell, J, Rivera, G and Silverman, A (2015) Imaginative Teaching and Learning in Waldorf Classrooms. *Research on Steiner Education*, 5(1): 94–114.

This paper was first published as Millar, C (2015) Why Research in 'Real Time' Matters. *Research on Steiner Education*, 6(2): 157–60. It is reprinted here with the editor's permission.

Suggested further reading

Atkins, L and Wallace, S (2012) *Qualitative Research in Education*. London: Sage/BERA.
Really clear and readable. Includes useful case studies.

Baumfield, V, Hall, E and Wall, K (2013) *Action Research in Education: Learning Through Practitioner Enquiry*. London: Sage.
Very readable and fully grounded in experience of actual classroom research.

Boyd, P, Hymer, B and Lockney, K (2015) *Learning Teaching: Becoming an Inspirational Teacher*. Northwich, Cheshire: Critical Publishing.
An insightful guide towards becoming an inspirational teacher, advocating a stance of continuous inquiry.

Clough, P and Nutbrown, C (2012) *A Student's Guide to Methodology*. 3rd ed. London: Sage.
An accessible guide to research methodology that includes examples from real research.

Cochran-Smith, M and Lytle, S L (2009) *Inquiry as Stance: Practitioner Research for the Next Generation*. New York: Teachers College Press.
A collection of accounts of practitioner research – some unusual and often emancipatory methodology.

Dadds, M and Hart, S (2001) *Doing Practitioner Research Differently*. London: RoutledgeFalmer.
The first five chapters are especially valuable because they argue for inquiry as stance and for critical inquiry by teachers.

Denscombe, M (2010) *Ground Rules for Social Research: Guidelines for Good Practice*. 2nd ed. Maidenhead: McGraw-Hill/Open University Press.
A thorough basic primer, not exclusively about qualitative research.

Hopkins, D (2008) *A Teacher's Guide to Classroom Research*. Maidenhead: Open University Press.
A systematic and straightforward guide to assist teachers to carry out research in their own classrooms.

Kemmis, S (2006) Participatory Action Research and the Public Sphere. *Educational Action Research*, 14(4): 459–76.
A useful warning of the risk of 'domestication' of teacher research: that it might become merely the evaluation of the techniques of schooling, rather than asking challenging educational questions

McAteer, M (2013) *Action Research in Education: Research Methods in Education*. London: Sage.
A useful guide to action research in the classroom that draws on case study examples.

McNiff, J (2013) *Action Research: Principles and Practice*. 3rd ed. Abingdon, Oxon: Routledge.
A standard text offering a clear explanation of principles and practice. Illustrated by case study material.

Mellor, N (2001) Messy Method: The Unfolding Story. *Educational Action Research*, 9(3): 465–84.
Reassuring when it all feels a bit too messy. Also googleable for a free online read.

O'Leary, Z (2014) *The Essential Guide to Doing Your Research Project*. London: Sage.
Another good basic overview.

Whitehead, J and McNiff, J (2006) *Action Research: Living Theory*. London: Sage.
A values-based and radical approach to action research.

References

Bloom, B S (ed), Engelhart, M D, Furst, E J, Hill, W H and Krathwohl, D R (1956) *Taxonomy of Educational Objectives: The Classification of Educational Goals. Handbook I: Cognitive Domain.* New York: David McKay Company.

Blumer, H (1954) What is Wrong with Social Theory? *American Sociological Review*, 18: 3–10.

Bruner, J (1996) *The Culture of Education.* Cambridge: Harvard University Press.

Egan, K (1986) *Teaching as Story Telling: An Alternative Approach to Teaching and Curriculum in the Elementary School.* Chicago: The University of Chicago Press.

Forster, E M (1927) *Aspects of the Novel.* San Diego, New York and London: Harcourt Inc.

Gottschall, J (2012) *The Storytelling Animal: How Stories Make Us Human.* New York: Mariner Books.

Gudmundsdottir, S (1995) The Narrative Nature of Pedagogical Content Knowledge, in Egan, K and McEwan, H (eds) *Narrative in Teaching, Learning and Research.* New York and London: Teachers College Press, pp 24–35.

Hagger, H and McIntyre, D (2006) *Learning from Teachers: Realising the Potential of School-based Teacher Education.* Maidenhead, New York: Open University Press.

Le Guin, U (1969) *The Left Hand of Darkness.* New York: Ace Books.

Lewin, K (1951) *Field Theory in Social Science: Selected Theoretical Papers* (D Cartwright, ed). New York, NY: Harper & Row.

Maykut, P and Morehouse, R (1994) *Beginning Qualitative Research: A Philosophical and Practiced Guide.* London and Washington: The Falmer Press.

Millar, C (2015) Why Research in Real Time Matters. *Research on Steiner Education*, 6(2): 157–60.

Milne, A A (1926) *Winnie-the-Pooh.* London: Methuen.

Newman, M (2014) The Tyranny of Academic Fashion: A Reject's Lament. *Concept*, 5(2): 1–9.

Proust, M (2006) *Remembrance of Things Past: Volume 2: Cities of the Plain, The Captive, The Sweet Cheat Gone, Time Regained.* Translated by Scott Moncrief, C K and Hudson, S. Ware, Hertfordshire: Wordsworth Editions.

Schön, D (1983) *The Reflective Practitioner: How Professionals Think In Action.* New York: Basic Books.

Stenhouse, L (1975) *An Introduction to Curriculum Research and Development.* London: Heinemann.

Xavier University Library (2012) Qualitative Versus Quantitative Research [online]. Available at: www.xavier.edu/library/students/documents/qualitative_quantitative.pdf. Cincinnati, OH: Xavier University.

Index

NOTES